PLAYING
FOR
FREEDOM

PLAYING
FOR
FREEDOM

The JOURNEY *of a* YOUNG AFGHAN GIRL

ZARIFA ADIBA
AND ANNE CHAON

AMAZON **CROSSING**

Previously published as *L'indomptable* by Éditions Versilio in France in 2021.
Translated from the French by Susanna Lea Associates. First published in English by
Amazon Crossing in 2024.

Published by Amazon Crossing, Seattle

www.apub.com

Amazon, the Amazon logo, and Amazon Crossing are trademarks of Amazon.com,
Inc., or its affiliates.

ISBN-13: 9781662511134 (hardcover)
ISBN-13: 9781662511141 (paperback)
ISBN-13: 9781662511127 (digital)

Cover design by Kimberly Glyder
Cover image: © David M. Schrader, © Naddya, © schankz / Shutterstock;
© Karl Hendon / Getty

Printed in the United States of America

First Edition

To my entire world:
My mother, sister, and brothers.
To Natasha, my friend in heaven.
To all women . . .

As I finished writing my book, I learned the news that the Taliban had taken over Kabul. Twenty years after they were driven out, they had returned to power. I was terrified of what lay ahead for my country. During the years that I was growing up, the threat of the Taliban had always been in the background, but I held on to hope. Hearing they were in power again made me lose that hope, and I had to find it once more. This is the story of how I found hope in the first place, and it is the story of the hope I return to again and again.

1

THE DAVOS CONCERT

Here I am: backstage, sitting on the steps, waiting for them to call me. I can see Najiba and Shekiba on stage in the front row on traditional Afghan drums, Gulalai and Homa on sitars, and Rabia and Fazila with their *rubabs*—traditional Afghan string instruments belonging to the lute family. The girls are all wearing traditional embroidered dresses. Behind them are Marjan and Samia on violins; my friend Nazira, with her piercing eyes, has her huge cello wedged between her frail knees. The others are wearing the black-and-gold dresses of special occasions, and red veils, which have already started to slide off to reveal their hair. My veil is red, black, and green: the colors of the Afghan flag.

In a few minutes, they will call my name through the speakers. Murmurs fill the room. Heads of state, government officials, leaders of the world's largest companies, economists, activists, artists, advocates for the best, and promoters of the worst all sit shoulder to shoulder. They have come to listen to the performance of a group of young Afghan women. They have come to listen to us.

Here I am. I'm about to step on stage and face an audience that, until a few months ago, I didn't even know existed. I will then turn around, my arms outstretched, whisper, "One, two, three," and raise my baton. In response, the girls of the orchestra will start to play "Watan Jan" ("My Dear Homeland"). A classic Afghan tune, my favorite.

I, Zarifa—the Elegant, in Persian—am eighteen years old. I am going to conduct the first all-female orchestra of a nation that has been at war, either with foreign adversaries or within itself, for forty years, and is described by the United Nations as the worst place on earth to be born a woman. My country.

This evening, *I* am Afghanistan. My heart is pounding, my throat dry.

I am experiencing a flood of emotions. We want to give a performance that will show the best of our country, the best of us. Even if we risk our lives by playing. It's a risk we all have taken ever since we played our very first notes.

Upon our return to Kabul, three of our group will disappear, married off by their families. I will have to resist my own family's attempts to hold me back, to coerce me into marriage, to take me far away from all of this.

But this evening, I'm not thinking about our return. Neither can I foresee the extent to which this tour, this trip, will shape my choices, and change the course of my life. What a journey it has been, getting to this evening in January of 2017, to this music that will ultimately carry me toward my future.

This evening, I am the bow of my viola; I am the baton leading the orchestra.

Tomorrow can wait.

◆ ◆ ◆

Dr. Sarmast had been unable to contain his joy when he gave us the news the previous summer: the female orchestra Zohra was to go on its first international tour, to Switzerland and Germany, in January!

At that point in my life, I didn't really know where Switzerland or Germany were. I'd never set foot in Europe, the faraway refuge to which so many of my fellow citizens had fled. Many people—some of whom I knew—had drowned in the Mediterranean Sea when they tried to flee to Europe from Afghanistan. Most of them so young, often teenagers.

They knew the dangers in trying to leave: life as refugees, assault on the journey, even death. But they were willing to face the risks in order to escape the difficult existence we were all experiencing in Afghanistan—terrorist attacks, poverty, the threat of Taliban rule—in order to build a better life for themselves and their families. The son of my mom's cousin died when he was just eighteen. I knew about these risks and losses even then, and that was why I didn't want to think about Europe at the time.

I was more familiar with the United States—or more accurately, I was familiar with Harvard. Going there had been my lifelong dream. But Dr. Sarmast, founder and director of the Afghanistan National Institute of Music—also known as the ANIM, where I had been studying for the past three years—was jubilant about our trip to Europe, even if the full significance of it was lost on me.

"We will play in Zurich and Geneva, then in Germany, in Weimar and Berlin. The highlight of the tour, the most important performance, will be Davos and the World Economic Forum! But I'm warning you. You will have to work hard. You girls aren't ready yet."

It was July and we had a little over five months to prepare. We listened to him respectfully, like we always did. We were so happy and excited by the idea of traveling to Europe, even if the name "Davos" meant little to us. We did not even know it was in Switzerland yet. In our minds, it was just the name of another foreign city.

Since founding the ANIM, Afghanistan's only music school, Dr. Ahmad Sarmast had taken his students on several tours abroad, including one to Carnegie Hall in New York. But this tour was unique: it was the first international event for Zohra, the all-female orchestra he had created at the Institute. Zohra was the first and only all-female orchestra in the whole country—and, I believe, in the Muslim world. Founding it was a real challenge in a society that is known for its strict conservative norms (even after the fall of the Taliban almost twenty years before), especially when it comes to the treatment of women and girls. The radical fringe has always viewed music as an offense to Islam, a sin.

As soon as the news of the tour got out, journalists and foreign correspondents in Kabul rushed to the ANIM to interview us. But Davos and this forum still meant nothing to me. It was the journalists' excitement that finally intrigued me. I first began asking the people around me at the ANIM, "What do you think about Davos?"

And they would answer, "I don't even know where it is . . ."

Was this event really such a big deal? After all, we, the girls of the Zohra Orchestra, had already performed in full dress at the presidential palace in Kabul. The first lady of Afghanistan adored us.

Nevertheless, one day during my lunch break, I snuck into the computer room and looked up "World Economic Forum." Photos of Bill Gates, Michelle Obama, and Shakira, taken in previous years at the forum, popped up on the screen, alongside the pictures of many other personalities. I read that around three thousand world leaders in politics, finance, business, science, and sports met at this snow-covered ski resort in the Swiss Alps every year to discuss world affairs and anticipate major upcoming challenges. But to me, only one name stood out on the screen, as if it were glowing: Michelle Obama. *Michelle* was going to be there!

I immediately ran to Dr. Sarmast's office to confirm it: "This is where we'll be performing, right?"

"Yes, yes," he replied, amused.

From then on, all I could think about was Davos. The other girls didn't understand my enthusiasm, but that didn't matter; I felt as though I had wings. I was utterly convinced I was going to meet

Michelle Obama. I was going to see her and talk to her. This became my obsession.

I was thirteen years old when I wrote the American first lady's name in my diary for the first time. Some people appreciated Michelle Obama because of her husband, Barack. I appreciated Barack because of her. Her beauty, her allure, her eloquence, her elegance . . . everything about her delighted me and distracted me from my daily life. Like any other little girl, I needed heroes and fairy tales. But it was Michelle Obama's commitment to girls' education that really made me admire her while I was growing up. To this day, she remains my role model. I drank in her words when she promoted schools, education, and studies. I listened to her speeches over and over again and could recite entire extracts of them from memory.

Watching her in these clips, I knew the exact moment she would raise her hand, point her index finger at the audience, and turn her head from side to side: scanning the room, furrowing her eyebrows, or flashing a huge smile. Whenever I had a smartphone or computer within reach, at my brother's house or at school, I took the opportunity to read her speeches and quotes and then posted them on Facebook. I especially loved the speech in which she explained that if she'd worried about what the boys in high school thought of her instead of focusing on her studies, she wouldn't now be married to the president of the United States. I knew everything about Malia and Sasha, the first daughters—and yes, of course I envied them. Not so much for their fairy-tale lifestyle but rather for their parents' beauty and strength. From that point until winter, it was the prospect of performing in front of this icon and that impressive audience that made it possible for me—just a young girl from Kabul—to power through the trials and tribulations of my daily life.

In those days, I had so little money that I couldn't even afford the ten afghanis (less than four American cents) it took to take the bus to music school. Instead, I walked for two hours every morning, from home to the ANIM, pacing along the damaged sidewalks of Kabul and crisscrossing the dusty city where high concrete walls had gradually sprung up in response to various threats and to protect against explosions. These T-walls—placed pointing in all directions, blocking residential streets and streets where important buildings were located—added to the chaos of the ever-densifying Afghan traffic. Every once in a while, vehicles were arbitrarily diverted for official convoys.

I spent two hours every morning on these hellish roads, in constant fear of a suicide bomber appearing out of nowhere or a car or truck going up in flames. Not to mention the men who would jeer at me as I walked by, adding to the stress of it all. And every evening, I did it all over again. My sneakers became so worn that I had to wear my little brother's and got terrible blisters on my feet. But I walked, I cried, and I trod along in the cold, repeating to myself: "Okay, Zarifa, it's hard, but you're going to meet Michelle Obama, you're going to perform in front of her, and you're going to show the world the wonderful parts of Afghanistan—the music, the culture—that are currently hidden by war, bombs, and the Taliban. You're going to show them the beautiful Afghanistan!"

The last couple of weeks in December, right before we left for Davos, were the hardest. Yet, despite the snow and the fatigue, the frostbite and wind cutting my cheeks, I never missed a single class, not a single rehearsal. I was ready to suffer because that's how much the opportunity meant to me.

Two months prior to our departure, Dr. Sarmast had announced on behalf of all the faculty that they had chosen Negin and me to be Zohra's conductors. We would lead the orchestra during performances and act as its representatives to officials and the media. Me and Negin—it was incredible!

We had first met at the ANIM. She played the piano, and I played the viola. Both of us had started training to become conductors, and we immediately became friends. Negin was slightly older than me. She was far more slender than I, and she had an attractive pale complexion that I—a stocky Hazara with dark skin and prominent cheekbones—envied. The two of us would be the faces of Zohra and our country on this tour.

For a girl like me—yes, I was "unlucky" enough to be born a girl!—orphaned by a father I never knew, raised by a mother who'd never had the chance to go to school, shunted like a burden from left to right in a family torn apart by tragedy, relegated to housework, the opportunity to perform in Davos felt like a miracle. It was an unexpected chance to see the world, but also to escape the hell I faced and the increasing number of attacks that marked our days. Since 2015, all those with the means to do so had been trying to get to Europe, to flee the threats posed by the Taliban and the violence besieging the country.

I never had any intention of running, neither before nor during the tour, it's important for me to add. I went to Davos with a single goal in mind, or rather two: meet Michelle Obama and play music to show my country in a different light, the best one possible. Thinking this way helped me to bear the harshness of my country's daily reality.

Throughout the autumn we rehearsed nonstop, but nothing was ever good enough for our teachers. We students were increasingly tense, acted aggressively even, if a girl arrived late. We felt demoralized by our teachers' comments. They always wanted more from us; they were real perfectionists. But whenever I found myself, baton in hand, in front of the orchestra—even if it was to play the same arrangement for the tenth time in a row—I was in another world. When I look at pictures from that time in my life now, four years later, I stop to admire my huge smile. I was always beaming. The teachers had recently confirmed my position as co-conductor alongside Negin and instructed me to conduct the first pieces of the opening concert. It was a great honor!

All the musicians in this unique orchestra had faced hostility, sometimes even death threats. When Negin first started playing music, her parents were forced to leave the province of Kunar and its green mountains, in the northeast of the country, to seek refuge with her in Kabul.

Her grandmother had disowned Negin's father, and Negin's uncle had sworn to kill her because she had "dishonored" him by playing the piano.

"If I run into your daughter on the sidewalk, I'll slit her throat with my own two hands," he'd declared.

We all had stories like that, some crueler than others. Out of all of the students, I was probably among the poorest, but my mother was willing to at least try to protect me from the rest of the family when it came to music—so long as I didn't cause a scandal. When I joined the school in 2014 and started playing the viola, she and her younger sister—my aunt Maha, who lived in Pakistan—were the only ones I told. The Uncles—my father's brothers, with whom my mother, brother, sisters, and I were forced to live—couldn't learn what was going on: they would have thrown us out.

For this reason, I could never bring my viola home. It was safely stored at the ANIM. We kept this secret to ourselves. Mom would cover for me, and in exchange, I would support her and my siblings with the monthly allowance, the equivalent of fifty US dollars, provided by the music school to students in need, which my mother used for groceries. This money for students had often proved the deciding factor for reluctant parents when Dr. Sarmast was attempting to convince them to allow their children to attend.

However, as the departure date approached, my mother didn't want to hear about the tour, and she stubbornly refused to let me go to Europe. Every time I brought it up, the conversation soured. And yet every evening, I begged her: "You know Michelle Obama will be there, right?"

My mother was perhaps more aware of who the American first lady was than anyone else in Afghanistan. I would constantly shower her—and almost drive her mad—with *Michelle's* speeches and announcements. But she stood by her decision, without explanation or justification. I'm still not completely sure why she felt the way she did.

It wasn't so much the idea of me traveling abroad that worried her—I had done that before. I think she was more afraid of me presenting myself before the world as a musician, especially since she had worked so hard to hide that fact from everyone.

Many conservative and old-fashioned Afghans still consider music haram: forbidden in the name of Islam. In 2018, a music teacher at the ANIM was denied a loan by the national bank of Afghanistan; the bank employee explained that the refusal was motivated by "religious concerns." In my mother's eyes, my playing music was a potential source of trouble. She has always been afraid of attracting trouble. She hasn't had an easy life and seems to dread whatever twist of fate could be right around the corner. So, she prefers to avoid any form of provocation.

The orchestra's departure was scheduled for January 17. With one month left, I continued to rehearse tirelessly with the orchestra, even though I still wasn't sure I would be allowed to leave Kabul.

One evening, I decided to take the plunge and go all out. At home, we'd lit the *bukhari* (a traditional stove) to combat the winter's freezing grasp on Kabul: vicious and unforgiving at nearly two thousand meters above sea level. As the stove crackled, I put a *teke*, a traditional bread made by the Hazaras, over the embers. The smell of cake, slightly oily and sweet, wafted from it as it cooked. The room was nice and warm. In this comforting atmosphere, Mom approached me gently.

"Is everything okay, Zarifa?"

"Everything's fine, Mom. How about you? Have you thought about Davos?"

"Stop it. When I say no, it means no!"

"But, Mom . . . *Michelle* is going to be there. I'm going to meet her, I have so many questions to ask her. This is a once-in-a-lifetime opportunity."

"And you're sure she'll be there?"

"One hundred percent sure."

I began explaining to her what the World Economic Forum was all about and why Michelle Obama was bound to be there with the heads of state, to talk about girls' education as she had done in the past. There was no way she wouldn't be there! And in any case, I couldn't let the musicians and the orchestra down.

My mother was finally moved by my faith.

"First, I have to meet with Dr. Sarmast, the teachers, everyone who is going with you," she said.

"You're welcome to come to the ANIM, Mom. If you want, we'll go tomorrow."

So, my mother came to the school three times that winter and was welcomed by Dr. Ahmad Sarmast. She needed to be reassured, and she was. She also appreciated these meetings where, for once in her life, she was treated with respect, as an equal, by a literate and distinguished man. On January 1 (not a holiday for us in Afghanistan), Mom and I returned to the ANIM one last time together. Trying to cover up the fact that she was intimidated, Mom wrapped an embroidered scarf around her beautiful face and put on a small black jacket over her long dress.

She sat in on the rehearsals. As we began to play, I could see her at the back of the room, looking both stunned and overwhelmed, pride emanating from her.

"I never got to go to school," she said afterward. "But today, my daughter is conducting an orchestra!"

Like a teenager on a school trip, she spent the whole day at the ANIM. She was ecstatic and at last granted me permission to go on the trip. Dr. Sarmast had known how to find the right words to convince her. From that moment on, right up until I got to the airport, I wasn't walking anymore; I was flying. I made a calendar that I kept under my *toshak*—a large pillow people sleep and lie on in Afghanistan—and counted down the days until it was time for me to leave. Every morning, as soon as I woke up, I would cross off a day. There were only fifteen days left.

Luckily, my maternal grandmother and my aunts who live in Pakistan visited us during those weeks and took care of the housework that I normally did. Everything became easier, and I completely devoted myself to the music. My aunt Maha, an artist who studies art and who is always well dressed, knew what Davos was all about. She was even more excited than I was. She cut my hair with scissors, framing my face with an asymmetrical fringe. She gave me lipstick and eye shadow and showed me how to use them so I could put them on before the interviews.

She also shaped my eyebrows and helped me pack my suitcase as she advised me: "Zarifa, when you talk to reporters, be positive. That way, when you return to Kabul, you will have earned a good reputation. Everyone will be proud of you."

"Yes. I hope everyone will be proud of us. The family and society, too."

"Be yourself. Those who don't understand you today will eventually understand you, whether that's tomorrow or in ten years."

I felt really close to Maha, who was, at only twenty-five years old, my youngest aunt, and her presence helped Mom and their other sisters better understand what was going on, and they all became excited for me.

On the morning of our departure, we were supposed to meet at the Institute at nine o'clock to get the instruments and, from there, leave by bus for the airport. I was already awake at five in the morning. I put on my favorite dress: a black one with a ribbon at the waist, black tights, and pink tennis shoes. I decided to leave my hair down. I made myself a cup of tea and lingered, checking my things twenty times over, so much that I made us late. My aunts Maha and Hani got in the cab with me.

Mom wasn't coming with us. She had to stay at home with my younger brothers and sister, but she kissed my forehead and said, "Go, and when you come back, I want to see you as proud as you are today. And be careful, don't fall asleep at the airport, you don't want to be left behind."

How funny. Did she really think they would forget me? An orchestra leaving its conductor behind at the airport, how could she think of such a thing!

"Remember to say your prayers on time. And most importantly, wear your headscarf properly at all times. I don't want to see a single video of you without your headscarf on," she added.

Though I did not know it at the time, in order to justify my absence to the Uncles and the rest of the family, Mom had told them I was accompanying the orchestra as a spokesperson because I could speak English: "No, of course she isn't going to be playing an instrument! She's just going to interpret for the others." The Uncles knew that I attended a school, they just did not know that it was the music school.

She had told a partial lie, and in this way, our honor remained intact, and the peace was preserved.

Of course I didn't get to the ANIM on time. We got stuck in traffic, trapped in a cloud of pollution, exhaust fumes, and smoke from the city's *bukharis*. I begged the driver to go faster.

"Listen, sister, pray to God and he will look favorably upon you," he replied.

When we got to the school, everyone was already on the bus. I ran in to get my viola. I kissed my aunts, and Maha slipped me a little MP3 player with all of Adele's songs downloaded for the trip—Adele was my favorite singer at the time. On the way to the airport, I put my headphones on and let my thoughts wander as I listened to "Someone Like You" and looked out the window. *It's okay, Zarifa, you're on your way.*

Everybody made it: all thirty of Zohra's musicians. Dr. Sarmast had succeeded; not a single one of us was missing. He had negotiated with each of the students' parents, or their guardians, to allow them to come on the trip. Today he says that close relatives like fathers and mothers were never the problem, that the only threats the girls faced came from distant relatives, from their wider circle. I'll never know how he managed to convince these relatives, because he now acts as though everything was settled far in advance and that the process of securing everyone's participation was fairly straightforward.

At the airport, people watched us get off the bus, noticing the brand-new purple jackets that the ANIM had given to us and, above all, our instruments. I had mine on my back. It was the first time I had ever gone out in public with my viola. I was so proud.

It was a crowning moment.

2

MUSIC

One night in 2016, before Davos, while I was sitting in front of the
TV with my brothers, my sister, and my mother, a television show
had played on 1TV, one of the most closely followed networks in
Afghanistan. The presenter of the popular late-night program was an
old mullah whose speeches families often watched during Ramadan. On
the screen, wearing his white turban, he had just declared that music
carried the risk of "drawing us to vice, rape, alcohol, and debauchery."

My mother sprang up and said, "Good God, Zarifa, what's going
to happen to you? I should never have let you study music . . ."

Luckily my brother Ali, man of the house at the tender age of fourteen, corrected her, laughing: "But, Mom, Zarifa has never done any of
those things! And she never would."

Now in late 2018, almost two years after the concert in Davos,
Mom was still uncomfortable with the idea of her daughter being a
musician. In my little world filled with such negative ideas about music,
I was considered a rebel. Impertinent, depraved. With my viola and
bow in hand, I was an insult to a society that was still stuck in the past.
I tarnished it. I pushed it toward sin. I was a "bad girl."

I was almost twenty years old, and it had been nearly that many years since the Americans ousted the Taliban from power after 9/11. Under Taliban rule, from 1996 to the end of 2001, everything had been banned. Women couldn't go out alone; they weren't allowed to go to school. Movies, music, concerts, singing, traditional instruments, and even cigarettes were forbidden. As I turned twenty, the Taliban were no longer in power, but that did not stop them from bombing our schools, our cultural centers, the streets of our cities, of our capital.

The Taliban hadn't come out of nowhere. The fundamentalist group originally developed in the countryside, in the Afghan mountains, where despite the Taliban's brutality, some of the population prefers the strict and rigorous order the group imposes, over chaos. This social order, which is still deeply rooted in Afghan society, requires women to stay at home, to remain subordinate to men—their fathers, brothers, uncles, and husbands—and to not aspire to education or emancipation. A part of the country likes the idea of bringing back this way of life, but without the violence. Many young people my age who are without work and without prospects in their future, or who simply feel hopeless, join the Taliban without necessarily understanding or believing in their radical ideas.

Still, my country has produced many great artists: the first painters of the Moghul emperors; the famous poet and philosopher Rumi; world-renowned writers like Atiq Rahimi; and modern superstars like Hangama and Ahmad Zahir, the Afghan Elvis Presley, a crooner whose love songs remain popular forty years after he died. When in 1996 the Taliban seized control of Kabul, they rushed to destroy Zahir's mausoleum, and in 2001, after they were defeated, his fans rushed to reestablish it with equal fervor and covered it with flowers!

I've always loved music. It makes me feel alive. My mother says that I was constantly singing when I was a little girl, so much so that people would joke about it in Qarabagh, Ghazni: the village where I was born. "She will be a musician," relatives would tease.

I must have been around six years old the first time she took me to Pakistan, along with her new husband. The young couple wasn't running away from war, as were the tens of thousands of Afghan refugees. They were fleeing his toxic parents, who hated my mother.

I was soon enrolled in a small school in Quetta, where my mother's parents lived at the time. The school was very traditional and conservative. We were made to gather in the schoolyard every morning, pray, and sing to the glory of the Pakistani "homeland." It wasn't my homeland, but I always volunteered to sing along with the others. I already enjoyed being on stage, in front of an audience. I also participated in dance shows during graduation ceremonies.

As I got older, my passion for music fed my dreams of the future and fame. Around the age of eleven or twelve, I decided I would become a pop star. I could see myself with a microphone in hand, surrounded by a crowd of adoring fans. I would regularly escape into this dream to get away from my glum daily reality—that of a child who was tossed from one part of the family to another, always at the whim of others' disputes and reconciliations.

I still don't know where this passion for music comes from. Nobody in my home was ever interested in music. So, the idea of me actually taking up an instrument was unspeakable! My family isn't super religious, but it is largely uneducated and very conservative. But fortunately, my mom—who never went to school and was married for the first time at the age of fourteen—never really saw music as a sin. I realize that she's less afraid of sin than she is of what other people might think.

When I was fifteen years old, she even let me sign up to compete in the *Afghan Star*, a very popular TV talent show. The program was, of course, condemned by the mullahs. But as was often the case, my favorite aunt, Maha, was hugely supportive. During one of her trips to Kabul from Pakistan, she found a vocal coach to help me prepare for the audition. Thanks to Maha, Mom finally gave in to my pleas. She even sold a small piece of gold jewelry to pay for the lessons and buy me a harmonium. I worked hard at my singing and sitar-playing with my teacher. He seemed very old to me and, therefore, respectable. But he tended to get a little too close and let his fingers linger on mine for a bit too long, and he stared at me intently. Living in an Islamic republic doesn't automatically turn all men into saints.

At that time, before we moved in with the Uncles, we lived in a tiny one-room house. It was just us: my mom, my two brothers, my sister, and me—no father anymore, no guardian or husband—as well as my grandmother and my aunts. We were free there, not controlled or abused by any male relative. I especially loved that my aunts Hani and Maha were with us. It also didn't hurt that an incredibly handsome man, slender and fair, sold samosas just around the corner! I would go and buy one for a handful of afghanis as often as I could, just so I could see him. But when I started practicing for the *Afghan Star* in the only room we had, everyone got on my case. We had neighbors with horrible tempers who complained bitterly: "Ah no, Zarifa, this isn't working. You're not letting anyone sleep. You'll have to stop . . ."

Two days later, the newly bought harmonium was sold. To replace it, I drew piano keys on a strip of paper so I could continue to learn. My ingeniousness impressed my teacher. As much as he leered, he was also the one who suggested I audition at the ANIM rather than the TV show, and for that alone I can't help but be grateful to him.

The ANIM, born a decade after the end of the Taliban regime, remained a miracle for my country and for me. Its founding had taken the tenacity, dedication, and determination of a single exceptional man: Dr. Ahmad Sarmast, a trumpeter and musician. Upon his return in 2010 from Australia, where he'd emigrated, Dr. Sarmast started this unique school and instilled it with two sacred principles that have governed it ever since: the coeducation of girls and boys—something that was (and still is) very rare in the country and generally forbidden before university—and the absolute refusal to define students according to their ethnicity. At the ANIM, students are Afghan before being

Pashtun, Tajik, Uzbek, Turkoman, or Hazara. We are all equal, and we leave the ethnic distinctions that poison and divide the country at the door.

I know this now more than ever: meeting this wonderful man, who offers girls and boys equal opportunities and rights, had a profound impact on my life. He believed in me and showed me that another world and way of thinking was possible. I was a big dreamer, and he supported this side of me.

This strict egalitarian principle—and the presence of music teachers from the United States, Australia, and all over the world, who each teach the violin, harp, cello, or piano—makes the ANIM a truly special place. Watching the students from his office window, Dr. Sarmast used to say the ANIM's tree-lined courtyard was "one of the happiest places in the country."

I thought it was, too. I am a Hazara, a long-oppressed and persecuted Shiite minority, one of the poorest in the country. We are still secretly or even openly despised by other ethnic groups. Our high cheekbones and almond eyes make us instantly recognizable. *Khalas* (maids), cooks, construction workers, and handymen are often Hazaras. I sometimes did not feel comfortable with the way that I was treated differently because of my appearance. But deep down I have loved my almond eyes and my cheekbones, and my dimple that accents them, for the way they helped me feel and appreciate Hazara beauty.

My mother's side of the family is from Ghazni Province, which is situated southwest of Kabul and is one of the Hazaras' enclaves. This area is also home to many Pashtuns, but the two groups generally mix as little as possible. The province is unstable, so my family rarely went back until 2020 when, fleeing the Covid-19 pandemic that was plaguing the capital, my mother, brothers, and sister found refuge there.

The road to access the area is unpredictable, and Taliban attacks were frequent. Once, a close relative of my father's was kidnapped while traveling this road. His body was found in terrible shape. He had been tortured to death. There was also the story of nine-year-old Tabasum, who was beheaded by the Taliban along with six other travelers in Ghazni in 2015. Every time I heard a story like this—about a Hazara who was killed for being Hazara—I asked: "Why? Why are they killing us?" I wondered what it was about us that made them uncomfortable. Was it the different shape of our eyes? I never understood the hate behind these killings.

The largest Hazara province is definitely Bamyan in central Afghanistan, where in 2001 the Taliban destroyed the giant Buddhas that were carved into the pink cliffs. They considered them to be "contrary to Islam" and wanted to erase all traces of Afghanistan's Buddhist past. To this day, farmers who plow the soil to reap potatoes mourn their giant Buddhas as one mourns loving parents.

With the exception of Herat, a large city in the west that benefits from its proximity to Iran, the Hazara regions have always been poor and neglected by the central government. In the hope of improving their futures, the Hazaras invest all they can in their children's education, making them the most open-minded and tolerant community in the country. My family isn't the best example, but it is among the Hazaras that you will find the first female cyclists, rock climbers, judokas, and swimmers, as well as most of the highest-placed candidates for the Kankur, the national university entrance exams. It is often Hazara girls who test and push back the boundaries of what is considered "acceptable" behavior, which doesn't help us gain respectability or make us more likable—except among some educated Afghans and foreigners. These girls who are rebelling are also fighting to change a culture that has been damaged by war. Afghans have a beautiful culture. Unfortunately, much of that beauty is hidden because of war, widespread illiteracy, and a lot of hate.

In fact, the first day I arrived at the music institute, the caretaker standing at the entrance stared at me and blocked my path, saying: "Go away, shoo, you don't belong here!" He is Pashtun. I am Hazara. Only once I became a conductor did he start welcoming me with a smile.

The ANIM is a family in itself. They opened their arms to me and helped me grow. For me, the ANIM is also a cocoon. It's where I met my first real friends, girls like Nazira and Negin, but also (and this is so rare in my country) boys like Samir, Samim, and Shiraz. The four of us were inseparable during the day, although it was impossible to see each other outside of school. Brought together by laughter and the good sense of humor we shared, we quickly identified a common urge to dream and break the rules. I liked them because they treated me as an equal, regardless of my gender.

For Dr. Ahmad Sarmast, music demanded an unwavering and unmitigated commitment. A devotion, one might say. In exchange, his students received a full education, from primary through to high school, plus compulsory English and musical culture classes. Each year, a third of the spots were reserved for girls and another third for destitute children—street workers and orphans. Wahidullah had been selling chewing gum to drivers in Kabul traffic when he arrived at the age of eleven, brought by the NGO Save the Children. The ANIM turned the pale, skinny boy into a bright young man and an accomplished pianist who later attended Kabul University, which had an agreement with the ANIM to take on its best students. Everyone from the ANIM had a shot to get into the university, because admissions were determined by audition. And the poorest among us, as I mentioned previously, also got fifty dollars a month—a way of guaranteeing the support of the potential students' parents.

Unless they come from the privileged and well-educated minority, everything in this country is always harder for girls. If a boy wants to become a musician, but his family disapproves, he can insist and insist, and he will eventually win, even if he has to find creative ways to get what he wants. But it's more difficult for girls to slip away between school and home, to find a job to pay for lessons or instruments, to find the time to practice, because girls need to carry out domestic chores at home. As for rehearsing in the evening at a friend's house? Forget it!

Dr. Sarmast wanted to use music as a tool to emancipate girls—a goal that earned him as much respect internationally as it did hostility in his own country. In late 2014, a couple months after my arrival at the ANIM, he almost lost his life for his belief in his students; he was seriously wounded in a suicide attack at the French cultural center in Kabul, where the traditional ANIM boys' orchestra had been scheduled to perform after a play. The play had barely begun when a fourteen- or fifteen-year-old boy, sitting in one of the front rows, set off his suicide vest, having bypassed the security checks. From the wings, my friends heard a big *boom*. They thought it was part of the show at first, but they soon enough heard the injured crying out for help.

I was at home that night. My family was watching a Turkish TV show when I received a call from a classmate who was in tears. The first thing I did was try to call my friend Samir. He'd thought initially that Samim had been hurt, but the blood on Samim's clothes turned out not to be Samim's, and both of them had managed to get out while many other musicians remained trapped inside. Nobody had seen Dr. Sarmast. It took an hour and a half for me to find out that he had been gravely injured during the explosion and had needed to be evacuated. He was unconscious but alive.

I remember that on that night, selfishly, I thought of only one thing: if Dr. Sarmast were to die, it would be the end of the ANIM, the end of music in my country. The end of my dreams.

Dr. Ahmad Sarmast was transferred to Australia, his second home, the country that had offered him and his family asylum decades earlier, in 1994, first from the war and then the Taliban. The doctors extracted numerous pieces of metal that were lodged in his brain. The explosion's blast had burst his eardrums and made him temporarily deaf—a devastating loss for a musician. However, that said, Beethoven, my favorite musician, was deaf.

"For months I felt like a symphonic orchestra was playing deep in my head," Dr. Sarmast used to tell us. He ended up recovering from his injuries but still has trouble hearing out of his left ear. The students know this and tend to talk to him from his right side.

A couple months after the attack, documents recovered from an arrest of Taliban members confirmed that Dr. Sarmast had been the suicide bomber's target. However, the terrible trauma of that event, and the fact that he knew he was a marked man, did not stop Dr. Ahmad Sarmast from starting Zohra a couple of years later.

"The girls wanted me to do it. All of them came to me and said, 'We want to play together, just us,'" he insisted when he explained.

And so, Zohra became the country's first exclusively female orchestra. Its young members were regularly prevented from playing in Afghanistan due to the country's violence and cultural taboos, but they were frequently invited to perform abroad.

"The name 'Zohra' is an homage to the Persian goddess of love, art, and beauty," Dr. Sarmast would explain, his eyes twinkling. This, of course, only added insult to perceived injury; he liked thumbing his nose at the extremists at any opportunity. Evidently, this was too much for the Taliban to handle. In a press release, they vowed to take down this man who was "corrupting the country," and, this time, they swore, they wouldn't fail. These promises were repeated in 2015 and then at the end of 2017. These weren't veiled threats, unclear and vague; on the contrary, they were extremely specific. They mostly came from a formidable and efficient terrorist mafia group affiliated with the Taliban. The security provisions were reinforced again, and the tall walls that protected the school, like those at the vast majority of institutions known to be Taliban targets, were covered in barbed wire and security cameras and given a bulletproof and blast-proof sliding gate. Only preapproved visitors were allowed in.

I wasn't aware of such dangers before I joined the music school. Even though I knew our city was frequently the target of attacks, I was, like all teenagers, focused on my little world and its problems, my family, my friends, my school, my dreams. But as soon as I found out that the ANIM existed, getting admitted was all I could think about. I, quite literally, forced my way in, despite my lack of experience and training.

My first encounter was not promising. I was only sixteen, but already too old to audition—the ANIM recruited children from nine years old and kept them on as students until they were eighteen or nineteen, at the end of secondary school.

Dr. Sarmast told me, very directly: "It's too late. There's too much to do to catch up to the students your age. That said, if you'd like to, you can sit in on our classes next winter, just to learn." He was not prepared to take me on as a future professional musician, he was only willing to let me participate.

But when I feel passionate about something, I don't give up, no matter how seemingly unreasonable my goal.

I begged him, my hands clasped together: "Please, give me a chance, I won't let you down."

He looked uncomfortable. Melodrama wasn't his sort of thing.

"Stop that! Well, if this is what you want, you have three months to catch up on the syllabus and pass an audition. Not a day more!"

I don't think he believed I could do it. He wanted to discourage me. For the next three months, I did nothing but study music theory, rhythm and time, Chopin, Beethoven. I chose to play the flute at my audition, but not because I liked it. It was a tactical choice. My sitar teacher's intentions may have been innocent. Still, I was uncomfortable with the way he touched my hand when shaping it on the sitar, and I didn't want to go back to him. The flute seemed the easiest instrument to learn quickly, so that was the instrument I chose. To be honest, I didn't really know what other instruments existed, besides the sitar and flute. It proved a good choice. My flute teacher Ustad Shefta was like an angel. I felt safe with him, and he did more than just teach me music theory; he became one of the first of many important father figures to me.

In three months, I managed to power through a syllabus of material typically learned over four years. I had no musician at home to guide me through the process. All I had was my obsession. I talked to nobody, saw none of my friends, stopped going to school, and helped as little as possible at home. I thought, breathed, and dreamed music. That's all I did during those twelve weeks: I learned, I practiced, I drank, I ate—and I slept a bit, too.

Incredibly, I did it! I had my audition in front of a panel of four teachers and was accepted into the program. Two months later, I put the flute aside and took up the viola. The first time I'd heard my teacher, William Harvey, playing his viola, I'd felt a profound sense of well-being come over me. It was love at first sight—or at first hearing. After assiduously pleading with the school's string teachers, I was given permission to join their classes. Dr. Sarmast hesitated, but the teachers all supported me enthusiastically.

"What have you done to them?" he asked. "Because they all love you."

The power of aspiration! The viola, the tenor of string instruments that sits between the violin and the cello, quickly found its way into my heart. Its deep tessitura became my confidant, my best friend.

From then on, all I did was work, work, work.

3

TRAVEL

I know how to fight to accomplish my goals and passions, for the sake of what matters to me. Traveling is necessary to this process because it is the first step to freedom.

When our Davos tour started, I realized I had only been out of the country three times—not including the extended stays with family or at my grandmother's house in Pakistan, which didn't really count to me as "traveling." Though it was certainly notable that I had gone. Such trips may not seem like much to young Westerners, who are often used to globe-trotting, but they are quite exceptional for young Afghans. Especially for a girl, and one with my background. Usually only the wealthy get to travel and study abroad, to India or Pakistan, or if they can get a visa, to Europe and the United States.

To satisfy my curiosity about the world, I had jumped on every opportunity that was offered, or at least presented, to me, and spent time browsing the internet whenever I could to find such opportunities. Through these efforts, I seized the chance to take an English course offered by the American Embassy in Afghanistan to students attending the ANIM. It entailed spending a month in Antalya, Turkey, in the spring of 2015—my first trip outside the region and the first time I saw the sea!

Then in the summer of 2016, I found, through Facebook, the Yale Young Global Scholars (YYGS) program: an incredible three-week learning opportunity created for young people around the world and held at Yale University. This time, the trip had nothing to do with the ANIM. I worked as hard as I could on my application, determined to secure a place at all costs. I had just turned eighteen when I found out I had been accepted. It was hard to believe, but I had made the cut and would be going to the United States!

I was ecstatic, but also a little panicked: there was no way I could afford to go. At no point had I considered the cost of the trip. As soon as the euphoria of my acceptance passed, I realized all my work had been for nothing. But my luck changed thanks to the assistance of one of my viola teachers, Jennifer Moberg, who was American. Jennifer had been involved with my application from the beginning, and she'd even helped me apply using her computer. She had been the one to call me into her room and say, "You've been accepted, Zarifa!" We had both cried. She knew how much I wanted to go to the United States, and she and some of her colleagues managed to raise the money for my ticket to New York: a gesture of pure generosity and support. Still today, every time I think about it, I want to hug them.

Americans see Afghanistan as the land of the Taliban, the country that harbored Osama bin Laden as he planned the attacks on the World Trade Center. It's also seen as the land of poppies, supplying opium to produce heroin. But few people in the United States had ever met anyone from my country. I was, in fact, the only Afghan in the program at Yale, surrounded by international students from all around the world: France, China, Bulgaria, Brazil . . . What other Afghan family would have chosen to send a girl so young, on her own, to America?! I enjoyed every minute, every second, of those three weeks. And each memory is deeply engraved in my mind.

Beyond my excitement at being there, Yale was a place where I felt incredibly safe, where nobody could hurt me and nothing bad could happen to me. I would lie on the campus lawns in the middle of the night and look at the stars. I felt calm, my mind at ease in a world at peace. I wasn't scared of wearing the beautiful blue shirt my teacher had gifted me with blue jeans and my white sneakers. I felt no fear that someone might harass me. There was a spaciousness in my soul that I felt deeply. I didn't have to cover my hair. The freedom from constraints was liberating. I was truly happy. My English was still rough, and I didn't always feel I could express myself as well as I would have liked to. I am normally very communicative. But I observed everything—it was all so new to me.

One night, at the laundromat, I came across a couple kissing. I was terribly embarrassed. I closed my eyes and tried to go past them, hugging the walls, hoping they wouldn't notice me. Another time, I asked a student about the symbol he wore around his neck. He told me it was a Star of David. He was Christian, but he wore it out of solidarity for the Jews who had suffered so terribly during the Second World War. I had so much to learn . . .

Everything surprised me. These young people led completely different lives from those in Afghanistan, far from the war there. It was at Yale that I first gauged the interest, and above all the curiosity, that my country aroused in others. I realized that Afghanistan did not have a good reputation, and that this made the presence of someone like me on campus all the more unusual. I stood out from everyone else, but my classmates kindly took me under their wing.

The truth is, I am open-minded, and although the war damaged many things in my country—including culture, tradition, and a belief in the value of education and freedom and equality—those things still live inside me. Over the past few decades, war has chipped away at these values in my country. But I am one of the lucky ones, because I have been stronger than the war. And I am not the only one. There are many like me, and even those who are more modern and liberal than I am.

Still, every time I look to the outside world, I notice again just how different we are in Afghanistan. We aren't better or worse than others but very different. And the fact I understand these differences makes me seem suspicious to my countrymen in many ways. Even if I find it irritating and stifling, in Afghanistan we have a traditional way of life that we hold dear. Perhaps this is an attempt to protect ourselves from the wars and the successive foreign occupations that have happened in our country.

After the Soviets came the Americans and Westerners. We Afghans may sometimes envy the comfortable way of life these people enjoy, but we also distrust them; we still think foreigners want to shape Afghans into their own image. All those who have tried to control my country have paid a high price. In the nineteenth century, the British colonial army never managed to annex us; the Soviet army was defeated by mujahideens; and then it was the Americans' turn.

Starting in 2001, the war in Afghanistan became the longest war in American history. Afghanistan is a country of rebels. No foreigner can tell Afghans how to live or think. Despite the succession of wars that have unfolded in the country over the past forty years, the parents of its young people have managed to maintain their traditions—even if doing so within the city is sometimes more difficult.

Afghans are proud people. This is what holds them together. They are also convinced that no place else on earth compares with their nation's challenging terrain, its high mountains and steep, plunging valleys. I believe this, too, with my whole heart. I believe it and I love my country—so much. When I have been given a chance to go some-where else, I only wanted to leave so that I could breathe and study, so that my head would be in a better place when I returned.

In Afghanistan, not all traditions are good. For example, even within the family, women are expected to behave with extreme modesty.

We never show more than the tips of our feet or our hands, and it's rare to see a woman's ankle, or to see a forearm or bare neck.

Of course, after 2001, it became increasingly common to see university students and certain young women wearing jeans and tailored tunics, their headscarves resting carelessly on their loose hair. But even in the city, the blue burkas that restrict women were still commonly seen in the public sphere. For those who wear them, going out with an uncovered face is the equivalent of walking around completely naked. And even if they want to take it off, they need permission from their husband, father, or brother.

This modesty is—quite literally—a cover-up for a deeper pride, and there's nowhere this is more obvious than at Afghan weddings. The women really go all out, parading around in their most colorful dresses decorated with silk and silver embroidery, tassels, medals, and jewels, and wearing the most elaborate makeup—with a preference for pearly skin and smoky eyes. Beauty salons in Afghanistan aren't exactly known for their light touch, but in their defense, I swear, it's also the clients who turn up saying: "Go ahead! Don't hold back!"

Most men, from ordinary men like the Uncles and my older brother to politicians, favor the *shalwar kamiz*, a knee-length shirt worn over wide trousers. In the winter, they cover themselves with a *patou*, an immense woolen shawl that is either beige or brown, to protect themselves from the cold. Both items are beautiful, and I love them.

Personally, I broke the rules and allowed myself to take certain liberties when it came to what I wore, even though it often made my mom angry. We fought about it all the time—particularly when she would compare me to the "good girls," with their tightly wrapped headscarves and long tunics reaching their calves.

I, on the other hand, would set aside some money whenever I could to spend at the bazaar, where I would haggle relentlessly. I had a weakness for leggings, and I wore them with midlength black dresses when I wasn't dressed in dark shirts and pants. I had a bright pink pair of tennis shoes and a matching pink headscarf that I wore almost constantly. I would wrap the scarf around my neck, leaving the material draped behind my shoulders, rather than around my head. The veil was another constant source of friction at home. My mother, who was always worried about what others would say, begged me to "at least wear it when you're in the neighborhood," and when I saw the Uncles or we had people over. She wasn't particularly conservative; she was just afraid.

I'd first started wearing the veil in Quetta. It is common and traditional for girls to be told to wear veils once their bodies begin to change, because the veils cover up their chests. My mother always told me to wear my veil correctly when we returned from Pakistan. I was already almost fourteen then. Strangely, in Quetta, which is ultraconservative, I could sometimes do without it, but that wasn't the case in Kabul. My mother wouldn't let me. She forced my little sister, Najla, to wear hers from the age of eleven. Najla is even more rebellious than I was. I worried about her sometimes. She would argue all the time, and she still does. She hates wearing a scarf.

I obeyed without giving it much thought until I went to the Turkish coast for my English training course in May 2015. One evening, I went for a walk on the beach next to the hotel. Seeing the waves rolling gently at my feet moved me to tears. This rhythmic sound, which I was discovering for the first time, filled me with a profound sense of calm. I slid my veil off to feel the wind in my hair and on my face, letting this tranquil and powerful beauty wash over me. For someone living in a landlocked country surrounded by mountains in central Asia, the sea, the ocean, is a faraway dream. That night, I promised myself I would bring my mother to the seaside one day to look at the waves.

I stopped wearing my veil again in the summer of 2016, during my summer school program at Yale. My host family had taken me to New York City, and I remember walking, head uncovered, between the skyscrapers, intoxicated by the place. I again felt that freedom I'd felt in

Turkey: breathing in the smell of asphalt, my hair flowing in the wind as if I were an Amazon.

When my mother saw the pictures of me from that trip, she blew up: "Zarifa, you live in Afghanistan, you have to wear your headscarf like everyone else, end of discussion."

It was not long after my return from the United States that I decided to stop wearing my headscarf altogether. I turned eighteen that spring. I was of age—even if that distinction didn't mean much to a young Afghan girl. From then on, I didn't wear it, except in certain situations: if I was walking on the street in Kabul at night, during Ramadan, in my neighborhood, or when I saw the Uncles.

One afternoon in November, a couple of weeks before Davos, I was taking public transport, sitting in a minibus, feeling glum. At that point in time, nothing was going well at home. We had no money, and I was constantly being criticized by the Uncles and, even more so, by their wives. They also lectured my mother, saying I had too much freedom. Mom, caving to this pressure, was obviously making me pay the price by picking more fights and beating me more often than usual.

To make sure I was comfortable in the packed minibus—they always try to fit in as many passengers as possible to make as much money as they can—I had paid for two seats in the front row. At some point in the journey, my headscarf had slipped off without me noticing. I was looking out onto the road, wedged up against the window. The bus stopped and jolted in the traffic. Suddenly, I heard a man call out to me from the back of the bus: "Sister, readjust your veil. You're offending us and insulting God!"

Other middle-aged male voices chimed in. I could hear a hostile, disapproving rumble. There was no one to defend me—only one young man had dared to let out a long, heavy sigh. The power of a crowd. I felt humiliated by their taunts, by the fact that these strangers thought they could dictate the way I looked and acted. But I didn't react. I gritted my teeth. When I got off the bus a couple of stops later, tears in my eyes, I felt more resolved than ever: never mind the rude remarks and public insults, I would go bareheaded. The only exception would be in Davos, where I would need to make sure I kept my promise to Mom and avoided doing televised interviews or taking pictures with my head uncovered.

But what an outrage my choice caused! Away from the music institute, where students are free to choose whether or not they wear headscarves, I was shocked by the things people said on the subject, including girls and boys of my generation.

"You dishonor me!" spat a boy once who was barely older than me. "You dirty me with your crime."

My crime? Some of them even felt they had the right to come up to me in the street: if I wasn't wearing a headscarf, I was clearly *easy*, maybe even a foreigner. "Hello, how are you?" they'd ask me pushily.

I've gotten into many fights because of this.

One day, I pushed an overly eager boy into one of Kabul's putrid ditches: small canals approximately one meter deep, filled with stagnant sewage. He fell in, bicycle and all, while his friends just looked on, amused, but I still ran away as fast as I could.

Another time, things could have gone seriously wrong. It was getting late when a man who looked about thirty started following me. I got rid of him with a well-aimed kick.

After that, I got into the habit of keeping a stick in my backpack; it resembled a poker and was normally used to stir the cinders in the *bukhari*. I wanted to scream at people: "If my hair bothers you, look somewhere else!"

All this fuss over a little piece of cloth that, through no choice of my own, had become the symbol of my rebellion. Imagine how I felt when I found out that in the West people swim practically naked! I almost fell over backward; I was sure it was a joke. A friend of mine had to show me pictures of packed beaches on the Côte d'Azur in France and in Brazil (where everyone's buttocks are almost entirely bare!) before I would believe it. All those bodies—vanilla, strawberry, caramel—oiled up and bursting out of tiny swimsuits . . . could this be serious? Just thinking about it now makes me break out laughing.

Even when I saw photos of the American Olympic women's swim team on the internet for the first time, all of them wearing tight one-piece swimsuits that covered them up to the neck, I thought they looked indecent. I didn't dare show the pictures to anyone. I realized that even though we always watched the Olympic Games on TV at home, I had never seen the swimming competitions before. The reason was simple: they weren't televised in the Islamic Republic of Afghanistan! The day my country has an Afghan female swim team is still very far away. I know a Hazara who dreamed of competing at the Olympics. The poor girl learned how to swim all by herself and would train in tights at dawn, when the swimming pool was completely empty.

Still, I don't think I'd manage to sit on a beach surrounded by naked bodies—I'd die laughing. It's true, we're maybe very prudish in Afghanistan, but in this case, I think things can be taken a bit too far. I also recall my surprise—and no doubt my stunned expression—when I arrived in New York in the middle of July and saw a girl wearing a miniskirt and tank top at the JFK airport terminal. I couldn't believe it!

Compared to all that, the liberties I took with my outfits remained modest. I imagine my reaction is surprising, my naivety, too. I suppose Afghans' ultraconservative relationship with nakedness may seem exaggerated. But you must remember, I never went to the cinema, and when we watched Bollywood movies at home, if a boy kissed a girl, even if it was just on the cheek, my sister and I would close our eyes or look away, so embarrassed were we to watch such a scene in front of our elders. And when Turkish TV shows aired in Afghanistan, the sex scenes were cut, and any low necklines and bare legs blurred out.

All of this is why my cellist friend Nazira and I found ourselves in hysterics at one point during our flight to Davos in January 2017. We were watching the movie *Me Before You*. It was inspired by a Jojo

Moyes novel that I had already read, and I was explaining the storyline to Nazira while translating the dialogue for her. But on the plane, unlike at home, nothing was blurred out. We were flying above the clouds, the meal trays had been served, and everything was calm in the cabin when, all of a sudden, the innocent rom-com's protagonists leaned in for a kiss. We cried out in unison: "Noooooooooo!" and grabbed our pillows to cover the screen and the infamous scene.

The Japanese man sitting next to us awoke with a jolt and exclaimed: "Hey! Don't worry, ladies, I wasn't looking at you!"

Well spotted. What we dreaded the most was someone, worst of all a man, catching us watching a movie in which people were kissing. How embarrassing!

This just goes to show that, despite my mini-rebellions, I had no intention of provoking people—in fact, the opposite was true. This was the case even as I traveled to Davos, a trip that would change my life so much.

Beyond meeting *Michelle*, I wanted to make as many friends as possible and tell them about Afghanistan to debunk the prejudices people sometimes had about my country. But most importantly I didn't want anyone to pity me, in Davos or anywhere else: I wanted them to admire the young women in the orchestra.

We were all around the same age: between sixteen and twenty-two years old. The older ones mentored the youngest members, and the atmosphere between us was special, friendly, sisterly, "girly," even during the tour. I doubt any of us will ever find an experience like that again. Several of our guardian angels joined us on the trip: our music teachers and, of course, our father figure, whom we only ever referred to as "Dr. Sarmast."

We landed at the Weimar airport, in Germany, where a bus was waiting to drive us to Davos. I was one of the first to get on, and I sat right at the front to make the most of the view. I didn't close my eyes for a second during the nearly seven-hour-long trip. I completely lost myself in the beauty of the mountains and the scenery. Everything was covered in snow, but the roads remained clean—they had already been cleared. It all enthralled me. When we arrived, a group of men and women from the security team welcomed us. They were equipped with earpieces and microphones hidden in their sleeves, which made them look like they were talking to their watches. "Hello! Welcome!" they said. We felt like we were in a movie!

We arrived two days before the gala concert that would be a part of the forum's closing ceremony. On the first evening, we were due to meet some young Swiss musicians from Geneva's francophone music college and have dinner with them. But before that I was going to discover the joys of the bubble bath. I had already taken baths in Turkey but had never experienced one with scented foam! I spent an hour and a half in there. The bathtub was so big a person could fall asleep in it. Negin, my roommate, was getting mad: "It's my turn!" she shouted, pounding on the door.

At the buffet, we were introduced to Clara, Amandine, Nina, Sydney, and some others. All of them were so friendly, generous, and welcoming. The next day, we were going to perform our first concert together for the media—a rehearsal of sorts before the big night.

I had rarely felt so free, excited, and happy. Not only was I abroad, but this time, and for the first time in my life, I was abroad as a musician, performing with the orchestra. I put on my makeup and did my hair—with no headscarf, of course. Nobody was around to tell me: "Do this, do that, cover your head . . ." I was also sure, confident, that nothing bad could happen to me. There wouldn't be any inappropriate gestures or comments here, no hurtful remarks, and no threats or violence, either. Here, the possibility of a suicide bombing felt far away. The whole thing was like a dream, one I savored thoroughly.

That night we were greeted by Nico Daswani, the arts and culture director for Davos. This young father of twin girls was to become a person dear to my heart. He was the one who had invited Zohra to the forum, just as he had invited Yo-Yo Ma, Bono, Matt Damon, Shakira, some Sufi musicians, and various painters and benefactors. Nico was a beautiful man and a beautiful soul, and he is the one who gave the forum its cultural dimension. I asked him if Michelle Obama had arrived yet. He seemed a little surprised.

"I think the first lady is most likely packing at the White House," he said.

Having just been elected to office in November, Donald Trump was scheduled to take over the White House in a couple of days. The Obamas were moving out. If an American first lady were to come to Davos now, it would be Melania. I was stunned. I hadn't thought things through. I explained to him why I had been so keen to talk to *Michelle*. Faced with my distress, he told me he was sure that would be possible one day. Carried along by the whirlwind of discoveries, new encounters, and press requests, I pushed through my disappointment. I remained confident, convinced even, that I would have another opportunity to meet my role model.

After the "rehearsal" concert, I had my first interview with Reuters in a small adjacent room. I can clearly remember that the journalist was wearing a lovely purple jacket and lipstick—I was impressed by her elegance. Thankfully, however, I had no idea just how important Reuters was. (I now know it is one of the three largest international press agencies in the world.) I was then interviewed by three radio shows and two television networks. And that was just the start!

The next day, Negin, Dr. Sarmast, and I were taken to the media village to give more interviews and a press conference. My American viola teacher, Robin Ryzek, let me borrow a black dress because I had no smart clothes aside from the outfit I wore to perform. We walked through this immense hall surrounded by microphones and cameras. People handed us business cards, and we scheduled meetings: everyone wanted to talk to the Afghans. It was disconcerting—and intoxicating.

At the beginning of the press conference, we went up and sat on a stage with our names written in front of us. I had never spoken in public before, and certainly not in front of so many people. Even though I felt intimidated, I knew I had to use this opportunity.

Most of the questions we received were about our daily lives, the risks we faced as girls and as musicians in Afghanistan, our studies and musical references, our education, our role models, and so on. I was sitting next to Negin, and we spoke on behalf of all the girls in the orchestra. I spoke positively and explained that times were hard for us, but that this taught us to never give up on our dreams, never give in to adversity. Emboldened, I then called upon all the world leaders participating at the World Economic Forum to support education and to give opportunities to people in other countries to participate in music programs, just as they were giving opportunities to the girls in the Zohra women's orchestra that day in Davos.

I had the thought that Michelle Obama might hear me defending every girl's right to learn. I imagined that if she did, she would be proud of me, and the thought made my heart happy. Now I, too, had been given a platform, and I seized my chance. In the next moment, the conference's mediator commented that only 20 percent of participants at the Davos forum in 2017 were women and that this was something that they could learn from the conversation: to have better gender parity at the forum. The moderator next asked what I hoped Zohra could teach other musicians on our tour.

"It's really a great pleasure for us playing with different musicians from Switzerland and Germany," I said. "But I'm really happy because we are playing for the world, not just for Germany or Switzerland. Because the world is going to watch us, and the world is going to have a point of view about Afghanistan. I know that about Afghanistan, you guys have a very different point of view: like war, Taliban, ISIS, and a lot of other bad stuff. But . . . Afghanistan has a lot of beautiful things like Zohra . . . very strong women who are cycling, who were nominated for the Nobel Peace Prize . . . There are a lot of positive things going on in my country. There is war, there [are] bad things, there is violence against women. But I'm so happy that today I got the opportunity to give a very positive image of Afghanistan to the world."

I was determined to show Afghanistan in a good light. Doing so meant so much to me; it was the fulfillment of my promise to Maha and a token of respect for my mother, who had let me come here.

After I spoke, the moderator noted that our press conference was the first time that week he had seen the audience at Davos moved to tears. The journalist who had asked me questions also had tears in her eyes.

Later, at a different press conference, a journalist asked me if I had a message for my peers.

I told her that, yes: I wanted all the young people listening to understand how lucky they are. They live in a peaceful country, they go to school, they are allowed to study. I said I'd met fellow musicians from Switzerland and Germany here, that we had performed together, and that I was astounded to learn that in their countries there were hundreds of music schools, whereas we had only one; I was amazed that in their countries, musicians are admired and envied and their parents are proud of them. I encouraged listeners of the interview to grab those opportunities and work hard, not only for themselves, but for all of us.

As the interviews went on, I became more confident. I'd never dreamed I would have so much to say. But I also understood that we had to feed the journalists' curiosity and hold their attention; we couldn't always repeat the same words and anecdotes, and so as time went on, I had to speak less about music and more about us, me, and my ambitions. And so, the invitations from major international media organizations kept on coming.

I had just answered a journalist's question by talking about my dreams of studying law at Yale, Harvard, or Stanford—yes, the crème de la crème of the Ivy League, no less!—and becoming a lawyer specializing in women's rights and promoting access to education and the arts, when a reporter from *USA Today* came up to me. She wanted to film a video for their website. We talked for almost an hour.

I remember mentioning why I wanted to study law, specifically. I told her I wanted to work as a minister at the Ministry of Education, to help change the education system in Afghanistan. I wanted this because I believed so much in the power of education. I believed, first of all, that a good education system could teach girls to know their rights as women. Secondly, I wanted to make music a part of primary education for every child. Music had taught me to hope, to stand firm when life throws difficulties at me, and to accept humans around me simply for their humanity, and not based on their gender or ethnicity.

Only a ninety-second extract of this lengthy interview was published, but that single minute proved to be crucial:

"[In Afghanistan] a good girl is the one who accepts her father's word. A good girl is the one who never goes to school. A good girl is the one who washes the dishes and sits at home. And, unfortunately, I am a 'bad girl' because I go and study. I want my human rights; I want to do what I love. They've [the Taliban] completely changed the point of view of people about the arts, about the culture, about everything. And even about women's rights. That was the worst time [when] my parents and grandparents [were growing] up. They were in a tiny world where the Taliban was the king, and they were like slaves."

I was battling with my English, trying to find the words to express everything I wanted to say. I concluded with these words about empowerment: "I am really, really happy that I am one of those girls who is going to put the first steps towards this."

When *USA Today* posted the video on its website, it was immediately picked up by social media and gradually became one of the most shared videos on Facebook. Fortunately, I had kept my promise to Mom and was wearing my headscarf with the colors of Afghanistan. In that respect, everything was fine.

On the last evening, Nico Daswani came on stage to open the gala and introduce Zohra: "When I met Zarifa Adiba two days ago, she had just one question for me: Has Michelle Obama arrived yet?"

I was backstage, my heart pounding, my throat tight with nerves and emotion. I heard laughter in the room, and some people clapping, which reflected the audience's distrust and disapproval of the White House's latest tenant, who would take office the next day.

The applause and the enthusiasm at the end of the concert were beyond anything we could have dreamed of; everyone in the auditorium was on their feet. Up on stage, the musicians waved over and over again, trying to prolong this moment of pure joy and pride. We were deeply moved when we were handed bouquets of flowers. Dr. Sarmast joined us on stage and did something crazy, unthinkable even: he hugged us in public like the daughters we had all become. He kissed my forehead, and Negin's, too.

In our country, men and women only embrace if they are members of the same family, and certainly not in public. Men give each other great big hugs, but us girls don't even get a handshake. Years after the concert in Davos, a friend told me that long ago in Kabul, women and men used to greet one another with a hug and a kiss on the cheek. This celebration of friendship between men and women is just one more beautiful practice that's been lost in recent years.

After that unforgettable night—January 19, 2017—I often thought about how I had achieved my childhood dream. I had been on stage, surrounded by a cheering crowd. It was my first victory, a decisive moment, even if I still had a long way to go. As for Michelle Obama, I still hoped to meet her one day. In the meantime, she continued to inspire and motivate me.

We left Davos feeling euphoric and having been lavished with praise and love, our heads full of memories and our pockets and backpacks brimming with Swiss chocolate. In Zurich, Geneva, Berlin, and then Weimar, we played concert after concert, singing in the bus, sharing our feelings and our excitement, and, in my case, often reading. I had brought with me a thick book, Dostoyevsky's *Crime and Punishment*, which I found a little dry. But the atmosphere was definitely festive! In Afghanistan, we almost never had the opportunity to travel like this. As free spirits.

In Zurich, Nazira and I shared a room with bunk beds. She was on the top bunk, and I was on the bottom, and we both slept with our instruments. "I'm holding my *boyfriend* in my arms!" she murmured on the first morning.

We laid them down in front of us and pretended to kiss them. Chaste young girls' love for a forbidden fruit. What a laugh.

When we arrived in Berlin, Dr. Sarmast handed me his phone—before we left, he had asked us to leave ours behind at home. Not that this rule affected me, I didn't have one! The others had gone to his office to plead for mercy . . . in vain! He didn't want to see them with their noses glued to their screens. Suddenly, I heard Mom's voice in faraway Kabul: "We saw you on TV, Zarifa! You spoke very well. The Uncles are proud of you. You are a credit to us all, my girl."

I hung up, ecstatic. Had the gamble paid off? Did the family finally know? Did they understand that I was a musician and that I was conducting the orchestra? Had I gotten them to appreciate music, respect my decisions? It felt as if a weight had been taken off my chest: I no longer experienced a deep-rooted, constant fear of being judged and criticized. That suffocating burden was now disintegrating, and I was free. I turned to Dr. Sarmast straightaway to share the good news. He had fought tirelessly to bring all the girls on tour and leave no one behind.

My luck definitely seemed to be changing! Despite the intoxicating feeling of success, we still had one problem: we were hungry. Some of my friends were very skinny—real twigs—and they, in particular, were suffering. What? Starving? In Switzerland? In Germany? We'd had our very first cheese fondue in Geneva, and, that night, I'd realized I was stuffed! But it wasn't always the case that I felt full on that trip.

In Afghanistan, a meal means rice, cooked in oil if possible. We are accustomed to saying that fat is a sign of love: the more oil there is on your plate, the more you are loved! But joking aside, most of our traditional recipes are indeed based on rice, to which we typically add vegetables or meat, like the tasty *qabuli*, for example. A meal also means tea. There's always a plate of rice and a cup of tea prepared for the odd traveler or foreigner that comes by. And if a person has the means, some mutton or goat. So, the copious plates of food served to us during our trip bewildered us. They were too sophisticated, probably. I wanted to try everything: the salads, the soups, the fish, but I admit I rarely liked what I ate. The other girls generally refused to try dishes they were not familiar with. People often say that Afghans tend to stay with other Afghans when they're abroad, eating in Afghan restaurants to cure their homesickness.

And that's what we did. There weren't any Afghan restaurants in Weimar, but our teachers found us an Indian restaurant, which served food very similar to what we ate at home. You wouldn't believe how many plates of rice and curry we shoveled down that night. We ate as if we needed to make up for days of deprivation and decades of hunger and scarcity before that! Imagine the scene: thirty-odd young girls, devouring their food with silent determination. That was the best meal of the trip!

In Kabul, a guard of honor awaited us at the airport. We posed together for the local press, our arms cradling bouquets. Some of the girls were met by their families, but the majority of us took a bus back to the ANIM alone so we could drop off our instruments. Mom was waiting at the school with my sister, Najla, and my little brothers Mansour and Homayoun. We rushed into each other's arms, laughing and hugging before making our way back home. They were happy to see me. I wondered if they could see how much this experience had marked me and the new perspective it had given me.

But as soon as we arrived home, reality set in. The apartment was freezing, and I was also struck by how pale my mother and the children looked; their faces were thin and drawn. I'd been gone for only three weeks. But usually, I received a little bit of money for the job of grocery shopping for one of my teachers, and I also was teaching English at the Star Educational Center. In my absence, my mother had found herself penniless without the financial help I usually provided.

"We finished all the wood," whispered Najla.

Every month, Uncle Haider, the head of the family, would buy five *seers* of wood for the two families. (A *seer* is a Persian unit of measure that equals about seven kilograms.) Two-thirds of this wood went to his family—his brothers, their wives, and children—and the rest went to us. In February, of course, the *bukhari* consumed wood very quickly; February was the coldest month of the year, and it snowed a lot in the winter of 2017. Plus, our apartment was situated on the top floor of the building and was badly insulated.

"You'll have to learn how to cut down. You can't always complain and use it up all at once," my uncle had replied in a severe, disapproving tone when Mom asked him for a couple of extra logs. He had this habit of telling her off as if she were a naughty child.

Seeing how tired they were, I dropped off my luggage and went straight out with my brother Ali to buy wood, potatoes, vegetables, and bread so I could make some soup while we waited for the house to warm up.

When we'd left to go on tour, Dr. Sarmast had given each orchestra member an envelope containing forty Swiss francs. This was a small fortune for me—I had obviously come on the trip without a penny. The girls were thrilled, even if some of them already had their own money. The majority spent it on scrunchies, barrettes, curling irons, skirts, makeup, and so on. Frankly, I would have liked to buy those things, too, but instead I'd handed the envelope back to Dr. Sarmast, asking him to keep it safe until we returned to Kabul.

I hadn't wanted to risk spending it. I was acutely aware of our needs back at home and was sure that everything necessary had been arranged and that I wouldn't need to spend the cash in that envelope during our trip. I was right. I'd considered buying chocolates for Najla—she had asked for them—but there was no need: we were spoiled with thousands of small gifts like the backpack I still use, given to us on our first day and filled with presents, including large boxes of Swiss chocolate. I will forever be grateful for such gestures of kindness.

Dr. Sarmast had complimented me on my good sense, and I'd contented myself with watching the girls unwrap their purchased treasures at each stop. I wasn't jealous; on the contrary, I was pleased. It didn't matter. I knew that one day I, too, would be able to buy myself whatever I liked.

But, in the meantime, we had nothing at home. We were constantly walking a fine line. So when we returned, I was very glad I had saved that pocket money and given it to my mother. It wasn't as if the Uncles wanted for anything. They owned several supermarkets and were relatively rich in this devastated country. But in their eyes, Mom and her offspring were not in their rightful place, and they didn't miss any opportunity to point this out. Their wives were even worse. If they had taken us in by choice, it was only to prevent malicious gossip and secure their spot in paradise—family loyalty certainly didn't have anything to do with it!

4

FAMILY

"When was I born?" My mother didn't understand my question right away, but I pressed on. "When's my birthday?! I don't know when it is!"

I must have been ten years old. At that point, we were living with my maternal grandparents in Pakistan, where little girls put on pretty dresses to blow out their candles on big colorful cakes, and I, too, wanted to celebrate my special day.

"I don't really remember," she replied eventually. "But I know it's written down in a Quran at the Uncles' house."

Let me clarify: when we mention "the Uncles" in my family, we're always referring to the paternal branch of the family. And we weren't particularly close with them.

When we returned to Kabul, I began searching for the book obsessively: it took me five years to find it at the house of my uncle Haider, the eldest of the family. When I finally got my hands on it, it turned out to be a large, illuminated Quran, which looked very old. Family members' dates of birth had been carefully recorded on the last page—everyone's, that is, except mine. Why? My mother couldn't remember the answer to this question, either.

Thanks to my mother's father, I knew I was born the same year as one of my cousins, in 1998. I knew nothing more, but I really wanted to know. I wanted to be able to celebrate my birthday, like everyone else. So, one day in 2013, as I was creating my very first Facebook account, I entered "May 5, 1998" as my date of birth. I had chosen that day, it was mine—my birthday.

I understood that at the time my mother had been neither expecting nor hoping for me to be born. But she'd never had a choice.

Ever since childhood, my mother has experienced adversity and has had to play the cards life dealt her. She has always been reluctant to talk about this, and it took me a long time to draw out the details of her sad story and reconstruct her past. Out of modesty or pride, she would only tell me scattered and disordered anecdotes. I tried to make connections, begging for information so I could pick up the lost thread of my birth and ancestry, and fill in the sometimes deliberately constructed gaps in our family history.

I learned that she got married for the first time at fourteen to a young man who was slightly older than her. He was a soldier, like my mother's father. Both families were poor, and so neither asked the other for anything.

My mother was the third eldest in a family of nine siblings. As children living in a drought-hardened village in Ghazni Province, she and her sisters would get up well before dawn and walk for more than two hours to fetch bread from the only baker nearby. Loaves were rationed, and each person could take just one.

"It was dark and the four of us girls would go together, to give each other courage. We were also able to bring several loaves of bread home that way. We would come back midmorning, exhausted by the long walk," she explained.

This bread was often the only food the family had on their table. My mother was poor, but she was beautiful, the most beautiful girl in the village. I once found a picture of her from that time. She was small with fine features, which she has kept to this day: round cheekbones; large, striking eyes; arched eyebrows; and a pale complexion inherited from my grandmother. All of these qualities were hers, along with a regal bearing she maintained despite the rags she wore as she traipsed through the countryside. She'd apparently never been intimidated by anything.

"I had nothing, but I was proud. Even the rich girls with their beautiful clothes looked at me enviously as I went past," she assured me.

Despite my repeated attempts to get her to open up, my mother rarely talked about her past, let alone her husbands. I didn't know anything about the first one, except that he was killed six months after the wedding, and that the mention of him brought a tender smile to her face. I would have liked to have a picture of him, because I had no idea what this young soldier looked like. Her first love, perhaps the only one she ever had, remained forever dear to her heart.

After his death, she managed to escape from her in-laws, who wanted to marry her off to another of their sons. That's how it is: once married, daughters become the property of the groom and his relatives. Her brother-in-law was even ready to divorce his wife to marry this beautiful widow of barely fifteen. Beautiful, but above all rebellious, my mother fled and sought refuge at her parents' house in the neighboring village. She was pursued by a band of armed men claiming the other family's due. It was a question of honor.

"You belong to us!" came the shouts from the deceased husband's family. "You can choose which one you want, but you must marry one of us."

The richest man in the family even came with some goats as a gift to convince her. But she was adamant; she wasn't having any of it. The men stayed in the village, spying on my grandparents' house, and following my mother whenever she stepped outside to fetch water, fearing she would get away from them.

One day, about a month later, they surrounded the house, determined to get her back. Accompanied by five armed men, her brother-in-law forced his way inside and threatened her parents: "We'll take her away, willingly or not. She belongs to us. You must give me your blessing."

Her mother was crying helplessly, terrified.

"So, I took a gun that was hidden under some cushions and shot at them—fortunately I didn't kill anyone! I knew how to shoot, like all girls who grew up in the countryside. I aimed for the legs," explained Mom. Weapons had always been easily accessible in Afghanistan; most houses had at least one, and most still do today.

The other men managed to seize her, but just as they were about to force her into a car, she escaped by throwing herself into the river, which was small and not particularly deep. She ran through the water despite the bullets whistling past that were meant to frighten her. She was never caught. Even though it was Mom herself and my grandfather who told me this romantic and extraordinary tale, I never knew if it was entirely true. Regardless, it is now part of her story.

After that incident, my grandparents accepted a deal with "the richest man in the next village." That's how they always described him.

"I had so many suitors, I rejected them all. And I couldn't understand how I had suddenly found myself married to an old man who was so wealthy he had offered my parents twenty thousand afghanis for me." Twenty thousand afghanis! That was a fortune at the time, especially for people of modest means.

My grandparents thus killed two birds with one stone: by giving her to this rich husband, they had preserved the honor of their insufferably rebellious daughter, who had been widowed so young; and with that money, they packed up and left their village. This was 1996. The Taliban, who are Sunni extremists, had just risen to power and controlled 90 percent of the country; Afghanistan's inhabitants were fleeing, frightened by the brutality of these bearded men who called themselves "theology students" as they closed schools, punished people for trivial reasons, and ruined the country.

We, the Hazaras—mostly Shiites—were particularly targeted. There are many tribes in Afghanistan that are Sunni, and many people from these tribes are my friends. They are not extremists, and they do not consider there to be anything wrong about people who are Shia. But according to the Sunni extremist Taliban, and to ISIS (the Islamic State of Iraq and Syria) as well, the Shiite Muslim religion is unholy.

The whole family fled to Pakistan, leaving my mother alone with her new husband and her terror and despair. "It was as if boiling water had been poured over my head. I was stunned, devastated. I had lost my dreams, my dignity, everything," she often told me. Her reunion and reconciliation with her loved ones, several years later, would never completely erase the bitterness she felt toward them.

In this way, my father bought my mother—a practice that was common, and not specific to him, or to her. And as a result of this sour and joyless union, I was born in 1998, in Zarsang, a part of the Qarabagh District of Ghazni Province.

In reality, my mother would have had nothing to reproach this second husband for, if it weren't for his age and the injustice of her stolen youth. How old had he been anyway? Far too old for a sixteen-year-old girl, that's for sure. My mother referred to him as an old man, and I always thought of him as one until I recently found a photo of him and realized he was probably far younger than I'd realized. The picture shows a handsome man who was undoubtedly no older than forty at the time of his death. Far from the ancient man I had imagined with such resentment. But, of course, to a teenager, the age difference was disgusting.

My grandparents confided in me that after the death of his first wife, my father became a widower with six children, the eldest of whom, Ahmad, had just turned eighteen. My father had sought both a new wife and a substitute mother for the little ones. Mom was the same age as his eldest daughters and was greeted coldly by the teenagers.

I arrived two years later. My mother didn't need or want another child. When I was born, she didn't know what name to give me. "You were so ugly I didn't know what to call you," she insists. "You were fat, hairy, and far too dark!"

What a curious thing to say to your child. But she didn't have any qualms about saying it. It was no surprise that she'd thought that way about me. She hated dark skin, which our society considered unrefined and provincial, as well as lacking the nobility and elegance associated with fair complexions.

However, a few days after my birth, once I'd presumably become smoother and less crumpled, I had become "so beautiful" she couldn't believe her eyes! She was finally proud of her baby even though having a girl as her firstborn was not her dream scenario. No one really celebrated my birth, but she decided that I suited her. Because I was born at the end of Ramadan, on the day of Eid al-Fitr—Festival of Breaking Fast—everyone advised her to call me Eidma. *Eid* means "festival," but it also means "gifts," and *eidma* means both "of Eid" and "my gift." It would have been a fitting name, but she refused. I had no name for three days before she chose Zarifa. Unbeknownst to my mother, who only spoke the local Hazaragi dialect, Zarifa means "elegant" and "graceful" in Arabic and Persian.

"I had heard that name once . . . I don't remember where. And I just liked the way it sounded," she admitted one day.

So that's how I became "the elegant," even though, at my birth, my mother had thought I was anything but that. The tides were already turning, however. Six months after my birth, my mother was widowed again. My father, who conducted trade in Iran, died of a heart attack during one of his trips. It wasn't until recently that a few more details were relayed to me in dribs and drabs by Uncle Haider, his brother: "Your father was buried on the return, it was hot. His grave was dug on the side of the road, not far from the border between Iran and the

Pakistani province of Balochistan. His travel companion took care of it." That was all he told me.

It was a rough ending for my father.

This time around, my mother didn't try to run away. Where would she have gone? So, she stayed with her in-laws—and with me—to raise her deceased husband's children. But she still felt stuck, condemned to solitude.

"Where could I go? I thought my life was over. I had a daughter. I would never get married again," she explained to me later.

This was not a happy time in her life. She wasn't even twenty years old, and she'd already been widowed twice. She lived in the village, on her in-laws' farm. They didn't like her very much, and so relegated her to the part of the house that overlooked the stable. The Taliban, who were in power in Kabul, completely controlled all of their lives, as well as the hearts and minds of the larger population. The Taliban would roam around the region in groups. No one dared to defy them in the villages.

"We were terrified of them. One day, I was in the courtyard with the women and girls of the family. I can't remember exactly what we were doing, but we were laughing together, maybe while we sorted the fruit. We were at home, after all! Some Taliban members walking down the street heard us. They stuck their heads over the wall and lectured us as if we were naughty children: 'Why are you laughing? It's forbidden! You should pray instead.' It was terrifying. We picked up all our belongings and rushed into the house. After that, we never laughed again."

She went on to tell me that when my father died, his brothers—the Uncles—behaved very badly toward their orphaned nephews. Uncle Haider himself told me much later that my father had actually been a hard worker; he had earned a good living as a merchant, and willingly shared what he had with the family. But after he passed away, the Uncles took for themselves anything they thought was useful or of any value.

"Even the radio with the cassette player our father loved so dearly," Ahmad, the eldest, told me.

My mother felt the same way as Ahmad. "That radio was the only thing that had real sentimental value for his children."

At first she tried to plead their case, and then Ahmad got involved. "They beat him with all their might," she said. "The girls were crying." My father's youngest son, who must have been seven years old at the time, tried to grab at the grown-ups' legs to prevent them from stealing the only precious thing the family had. "But they hit him, too," my mother said. "And he fell to the ground."

My father's brothers took everything—including the famous radio. They stole from orphans instead of protecting them.

There was still, however, the question of my mom's fate. Many widows in this country suffer greatly after their husbands die. Because people still believe that unmarried widows bring bad luck, these women are typically forced to marry a brother-in-law or another member of the deceased husband's family—according to this custom, the marriage saves them from dishonor and ruin. Or they are driven out by their in-laws, who also sometimes take their male children from them.

This happened to Leila, a distant cousin of mine. Her husband was killed in July 2016 in a terrible attack that targeted a Hazara protest in Kabul. This was the first of an endless series of massacres carried out by the Islamic State in the heart of the capital, which resulted in more than eighty deaths and two hundred casualties, according to official figures. Leila's husband had been twenty-three years old; she was twenty-two. Her in-laws kept their grandson and chased their daughter-in-law away, forcing her to seek refuge at her parents' house with her one-year-old daughter. Leila cried all day every day after that. She's never been allowed to see her son again.

My mother, however, wasn't chased out of the family home when her husband died, and she wasn't forced to marry anyone. She was, in fact, still the guardian of my father's children, and she was allowed to stay there until the weddings of Ahmad and his sisters, whom she called "my daughters" even though they were almost the same age as her!

Life was harsh and joyless in the Taliban's austere Afghanistan. But with time, and by necessity, my mother got used to my presence. From the time I turned three, she concentrated on turning me into a model child who ate neatly and made sure not to get dirty, even when playing with the cows. She saw me as a source of pride, a challenge. Like many children who grow up in an emotionally charged household, I instinctively learned how to keep a low profile and blend into the background. But my presence was still too much for her sisters-in-law and her mother-in-law, who even then harassed my mother and complained about me at every opportunity.

I must have been about four years old when the whole family left the village to return to Kabul. I have memories of this time that are both vague—I cannot place these events on a timeline—and incredibly detailed, shaken as I was by the startling brutality of the situation. Even now, recalling the cruelty that led to that move makes tears well up in my eyes. Once again, an argument had broken out between the women of my late father's family; Uncle Haider's wife, Mom's sister-in-law—one generation older than her—had lashed out at me, the widow's daughter.

"Zarifa isn't one of us. She's not part of our family!" she spat.

Wounded by them, Mom turned on me. I can still see her pushing me and shooing me away with her hands. As if I were a fly, or an intruder. She was beside herself with anger.

"Don't be like this. She's only a child," said a female cousin, trying to calm her down.

But Mom kept on screaming at me, holding nothing back. "Get out of here, go away!"

To this day, when I think about this incident, it breaks my heart. It must have imprinted itself on my flesh, branded me, to be able to still make me feel this way. I can see myself crying, sitting in my little dress on the front steps of the house in Kabul. Two cousins took pity on me and brought me water and washed my face. I ended up scaling the garden wall, hoping to take refuge at the home of Ahmad, who was living next door. But no one was there to open the door, to help me, and so I fell asleep, exhausted, straddling the low wall. Someone eventually came to get me. I don't know who it was. But I vividly remember the loneliness and abandonment I felt that day. I still sometimes feel like that. Mom drove me away. It wouldn't be the only time that happened. But since then, after having lived with her for so long, I have come to understand that she is capable of both saying horrible things to me and showering me with compliments.

Oddly, even though she was visibly struggling to fulfill her role as my mother, Mom took being a stepmother to my father's children very seriously. Understandable, maybe, because this position did give her a certain social status. But there were soon new problems to deal with. Sabira, one of my father's eldest daughters, had been promised to her cousin Basir, Uncle Haider's son. But Basir had fallen in love with Mom and proposed to her, sidelining Sabira.

"That is out of the question!" My mother had recoiled, terrified. "Besides, I have to get my daughters married off first!" Yes, she really did say "my daughters."

Ahmad, who was then in his early twenties, threatened him: "Basir, if you don't marry my sister, I won't marry yours."

This obsession with marrying between cousins is common in my country. Why? No doubt the intention is to keep things in the family and guarantee that honor is preserved. It isn't always the best idea, that's for sure.

Basir didn't give up. He decided to wait for my mother. But she stood by her refusal—that is, until after Ahmad and his two sisters, including Sabira, got married. She planned those weddings in minute detail: they were her triumph. After that, she gave in and married her third husband. That's how the tall, strong, and imposing Basir became "my father." As a small child, I didn't even know I'd had another father! Basir is the man I grew up with as a parent. Back then, he accepted my mother and me without question. Together they had four children: my three brothers and my sister, whom I adore and feel responsible for. They are the ones who give meaning to the word "family" for me.

This union, however, sowed further discord between Mom and the Uncles' side of the family. In the family's defense, the situation *was* chaotic. With this third try at matrimony, Mom, who had been the wife of Uncle Haider's brother, was now married to Uncle Haider's son. Haider's wife went from being my mother's sister-in-law to being her mother-in-law. From the outside, I guess it sounds a little crazy, but such arrangements are not uncommon in Afghanistan. Even so, Ahmad's sisters, Mom's "daughters," had a hard time accepting the situation. To top it all off, at that time, everyone lived together in the same family compound in Qarabagh, Ghazni. Later, everyone would live together in Kabul, too: though in Kabul, at least, there would be a wall that divided the sides where my uncle's family and my father's family lived.

To this day, when a girl gets married—even in the city—she usually moves in with her husband's family. It's rare for young couples to leave and set up house elsewhere. Mom had already been living with the family as a widow, and her situation was even more complicated because she had married a man much older than her. By marrying Basir, she was finally marrying a man her own age. She now became the family's daughter-in-law, although this didn't prevent her new mother-in-law (her former sister-in-law) from spewing her usual bitter comments:

"You're just a widow. You should be grateful that Basir even wanted you, you and *your* daughter . . ."

"Widow" was an insult that always devastated my mother: "Every time they would call me 'the widow,' it felt as if someone was plunging a knife into my heart," she told me.

Why heap shame and disgrace on widows' sad fates? Even now, in the twenty-first century, despite four decades of war depriving so many women of their husbands, the authorities ignore their existence and have no system for keeping count of them. They are invisible.

Uncle Haider's wife despised Mom so much that living together became unbearable. Mom had been married for almost three years when things reached a breaking point. She was then pregnant with Najla, my little sister. I was seven years old. Ali, her eldest son, was barely one. She couldn't stand being insulted and treated like a workhorse, being forced to carry out all the chores despite her growing belly. So we left Kabul for Quetta, where her parents and sisters lived. My mother has always said that we left for Pakistan the first time because of Haider's wife.

I don't remember much about our departure, but I do have happy memories from my time in Pakistan. Mom had made peace with her parents. My grandfather had a small grocery store and sold milk, yogurt, and cream.

In my mind, my grandparents were angels. They radiated tenderness and kindness, and I felt reassured by their perpetual smiles and their faces wrinkled from hard work. My grandfather would never take his cap off, and always pulled it down over his almond-shaped eyes. My grandmother kept her white headscarf tied tightly under her chin. They had two sons and seven daughters together. Having so many daughters was not easy in our culture, but my grandfather always treated his girls well. Though he married my mother off to my father for money, there is no doubt he did so because he thought he was securing her future and well-being. That's what I want to believe, because he truly stood out from the majority of Afghan men of his generation that I have come across. He adored my grandmother and frequently sang to her. He worked hard to secure a happy life for the whole family.

They lived in the Hazara district of Quetta. Hazara Town and Mari Abad were home to a whole community of people who had fled the violence of the Taliban. There were hospitals, universities, schools, and a bazaar. My grandparents' house had four bedrooms, an immense living room, and a large kitchen, all on one floor. Several vines laden with heavy, sweet bunches of grapes grew in front of the yellow door in the courtyard. It was a cozy and welcoming refuge.

Basir set up a small glazing and window business. With the influx of Afghan refugees settling in Quetta—people who didn't even consider going back—the construction market was booming. I went to a Pakistani school, the Perfect Model High School, where I studied in Urdu. Every morning, I would sing with my class and in front of my classmates, and after school, I would sometimes mind Basir's shop if he had to visit construction sites. I liked that he trusted me; it gave me confidence. Najla was born in Kabul, a few months before we left for Pakistan, and little Mansour was born later, in Quetta. Basir treated me and his children equally. He was my father. At no point did I wonder why I was the only one who called him "Uncle" and not "Dad." I didn't question it, nor did anybody else, for that matter—no adult thought of telling me the truth. But it didn't matter, I was happy. Sadly, that happiness didn't last.

I loved living near my grandmother and Mom's sisters, and after we'd been in Quetta for six years, I was about to transfer to an Afghan high school that taught in Persian, called The Noor High School: literally "The School of Light." Surprisingly, I've only thought of it now: Maybe at this point I should have seen the light regarding my parentage? For I passed the entrance exam easily, and, when it came to my registration, the principal checked my file and personal details.

"Is your father's name Mohammad Ibrahim?" he inquired. This was, in fact, the full name of my father, though I didn't know it then. In Afghan schools, children are identified not by their surnames but by their father's full name. I had always believed that Basir was my father.

I turned to my mom and looked at her inquiringly. She was frozen to the spot, staring intensely at the wall above the desk. She couldn't answer in front of a stranger. I sensed her discomfort and did not insist. I probably didn't want to dig any deeper.

"No. His name is Basir," I replied. I asked him to correct my file.

And just like that, without looking any further into the matter, the principal changed the record of my father's name. I kept my questions to myself—if I had any. What really mattered was not embarrassing or upsetting Mom. My intuition told me that there was a secret here that would be better left alone.

After this incident, life went on as if nothing had happened. I stopped thinking about it. But the attacks against the Hazaras were multiplying in Quetta; the city was becoming less and less safe. The cemeteries were filling up. My parents decided to return to Kabul, where the Americans were fighting alongside other Western nations to counter the Taliban's return to power after having been driven out in 2001. It was 2012 then, and President Obama, who'd originally wanted to withdraw from the war, had ended up sending tens of thousands of troops to Afghanistan in the hope that it would bring the conflict to an end.

To be honest, it wasn't the best time for the family to move back! But I think Basir wanted to reclaim his role of managing the family's affairs. At least that's what I assumed was happening. No one ever thought to talk to me about this or indeed about any other topic, for that matter. Anything relating to money was not to be discussed with the children—especially not with the daughters.

I can remember our arrival in Kabul perfectly. Ahmad, my older half brother, was still living in the house next to Uncle Haider's, with his wife and two children. The last time I'd seen him, I was six or seven years old. Now, I was fourteen.

We moved back in with Haider, Basir's father. Once again, the two family gardens were separated by a single wall, which was easy enough to climb when one used the ladder that was always leaning up against it. The ties of kinship remained deliberately blurred as the family introduced Ahmad to me as my cousin and did the same with his brothers and sisters. Very quickly, there was tension within the family once again. Was it precisely because Basir had wanted to reassert his rights? It was all beyond me.

I had no interest in Kabul, nor in the people living there. I didn't know anybody. I thought the city was ugly and hostile. Without the large veils worn by the women in Quetta, it lacked color. I was enrolled in the neighborhood high school in the west of the capital, where the Hazaras lived. But I had no friends. I was already missing Quetta, my school, my grandmother's presence, her soft cheeks and hands, and my beloved aunts, including Maha: my confidant and accomplice, who was always so elegant and cheerful.

At home, fights between Mom and the Uncles would frequently break out, and these were usually about me. They blamed her for my mere existence—it was as if I didn't belong to the family at all. Mom would avoid at all costs anything that could provoke the family's wrath. She forced me to cover my hair and wear a veil. At one point, a terrible argument broke out between Mom and several members of the family: my brother's wife, my uncle's wife, my mother's brother-in-law . . . everyone was involved. Had I been the cause? If I hadn't, I soon would be, as per usual. Their rage was terrifying.

I heard my mother scream to my brother Ahmad: "Well, if that's the way it is, you can take her back. Here's your sister, take her! Come on, Zarifa, leave. Go back to your family, I can't handle it anymore!"

Your sister? Your family? What was she talking about?

Ahmad's wife then started yelling: "But I don't want the orphan! I don't want her! If she ever sets foot in my house, I'll break her legs."

I didn't understand any of it. In my mind, Mom; Basir; and the other children, Ali, Najla, and Mansour—who were eight, seven, and four—were my family. My world was falling apart. I felt cold. I had always obeyed without flinching, especially when Mom exploded and lost control of her anger. But now, I was petrified. She disappeared and came back dragging a huge suitcase stuffed with all my belongings.

"Go away, Zarifa, I've had enough. I'm sorry, but I can't take it anymore," she kept repeating. She was rattled and white-faced. Was she crying?

Basir, "my father," had witnessed the whole scene without reacting. He obviously knew what was going on. He asked me if I wanted to leave. I wanted to cry out: "No, I don't want to leave. I really don't. Protect me." But I remained silent. I could barely lift the suitcase. It was as heavy as the millstone around my neck. Why wasn't anyone helping me? How could these adults just stand there and coldly watch me, immobilized by anger or embarrassment, and not react? I was only fourteen years old. Nobody moved or reached out to me. Nobody put an end to this madness. None of it made any sense. I learned one thing that day: when a person knows why they are in pain, they are better prepared to deal with it. But when the pain is caused by loved ones who do not explain why they are inflicting it, that pain burns even worse. Still today, I believe I might carry that scar on my heart forever.

Stunned and silenced by shock and pain, I went out into the garden and walked the few meters that separated me from my new life. If I wasn't Basir's daughter, who was my father? Who was this man I knew nothing about and that no one ever mentioned? A stranger, a ghost who had disappeared after I was born, yoking my mother to this resentful and jealous family. Why had no one explained these things to me?

The first night at Ahmad's was dreadful. The place where I was to sleep only contained a thin mattress, a pillow, and a red blanket. It was almost summer. I opened my window. I can still remember looking up at the moon and starry sky. Later on, Bilal bought carpet for my room.

Ahmad's wife was beside herself. As if she needed an extra burden! She already had three children. She was a pretty, elegant woman, with short hair that was always hidden under a purple and white flowery veil. She was still young but couldn't stand my presence. She didn't talk to me, only shouted, and referred to me as "the orphan" to my face. I was absolutely terrified of her. I stayed hidden behind Ahmad as she cooked dinner.

"Calm down, stop!" he said, trying in vain to appease his wife. "Zarifa is my father's daughter—you want me to leave her out on the street?"

But she refused to listen. Every chance she got, she would call me "the orphan," which was the worst insult anyone could throw at me. My mother was "the widow," so I was "the orphan," forever cut off from a father—and thus a man, a protector, an authority figure—which was all that could give me an identity in this country.

After that I quickly started to lose my way. I felt that I was in a dark hole. The impact on my school grades was obvious: I went from being the star pupil to the bottom of the class. I couldn't bring myself to do my homework anymore; Ahmad's wife was overwhelming me with domestic chores: "You need to get on with the laundry and cleaning, there are still the dishes to wash. There's more to life than studying. Hurry up!"

Nothing I did ever seemed to be good enough. She made no exceptions—even on the day of my school exams. After a couple of months, I stopped going to class altogether.

I no longer had any contact with my mother or my brothers and sister. I probably could have talked to them if I wanted to, but at that time, I didn't want that. I did not see them until many months later, at a family gathering at Haider's house. He had invited Ahmad's family, and they brought me along with them. But no one greeted or kissed me. My little brothers and sister kept their distance. Maybe they didn't dare speak to me. I felt like an outcast. When I saw my mother, the dam of emotion inside me broke open, and I began to cry.

I had put on a lot of weight. It must have been scary to see. During my months away from my mother and siblings, I had been unable to process my feelings. I had been unable to even cry. Food was my only source of comfort, so I would stuff myself to fill the abyssal void growing inside me. I might have become anorexic, but instead, I became bulimic. In nine months, I had gained over sixty pounds.

I was now fourteen years old and obese. I felt trapped. I had lost all self-confidence and no longer trusted the people I had loved more than anything. I despised my mother, who had abandoned me, and hated this so-called father who had imposed this hostile family on me. I hated everyone, including, ultimately, myself. There was no way out. What future could I dream of in such a world?

On the day of Uncle Haider's party, I sang one of the many songs I had learned during those months that we had spent apart, repeating them over and over again. It was about a child deprived of her mother, forced to grow up without her . . . Obviously—and that must have been my intention—Mom burst into tears. That was the trigger. A few days after seeing me all chubby and swollen, singing this sad song in front of the family, she finally acted. After a long period of silence, she came to see me.

She started a long and bitter negotiation with my half brother so she could take me back. Two or three times a week, she would come to talk with him. Ahmad would refuse, arguing that I was his sister, which meant that I belonged to him and needed to live with them.

Yes, girls belong to the men in Afghanistan. I don't want to generalize and say this is the way it is for everyone in my country, but it's often very much like that, which complicates everything. My brother's family didn't like me, they didn't know me, but I was theirs, so they had to keep me. Mom finally lost her patience and showed up one night with all the determination she could muster—which was considerable. She could be very authoritarian at times and would lose her temper if someone resisted her.

I remember her bursting into Ahmad's house that evening; it wasn't yet dark outside. Calmly, soberly, but in a tone that brooked no argument, she informed my brother that she was there to get me.

"You come to get her, but I know you're going to kick her out again . . . The next time that happens, I'm not taking responsibility," warned Ahmad.

"No, I promise. It won't happen again. This time I'm taking her for good. She's coming with me," replied my mother.

He tried to argue, but my mother was insistent, and he eventually gave in—his wife would certainly be pleased to see me go. Ahmad then took my hand and led me into the adjacent room. He asked me to sit down and listen to him. I did as I was told, exhausted after what I had just witnessed.

"Zarifa, you are our father's daughter. You can stay here as long as you want and count on me. Do you want to go back to your mother?"

I couldn't bring myself to say either yes or no. Which answer would get me in the least amount of trouble?

He gave me a final warning: "Know that if you leave, you can never come back here. It will be your decision."

I broke down in tears. What a heartbreaking choice to make at my age. I felt like I was nothing more than a burden, passed back and forth. Of course, I wanted my mother back, I missed her so much. But if I left and she kicked me out again, what would I do? Where would I go if Ahmad didn't want me anymore? I still chose to go with her. And I didn't see Ahmad and his family again for another year and a half.

What I didn't know then, and what I only learned very recently, was that Basir, my stepfather, was against me coming back. My absence had suited him, even if he never came out and said it. To convince him, my mother claimed I had some savings, a small amount of money inherited from my father, fifteen thousand afghanis—about two hundred dollars. Times were hard, and she promised to give it to him if he allowed me back. This wasn't actually true, of course—I didn't have a penny to my name.

"I sold my last gold necklace to pay for your return," she told me much later.

We girls are just merchandise. We are, like necklaces, goods to be bought and sold.

So, I moved again. My hastily packed suitcase was thrown into the trunk of Basir's car, and we headed for the house where he and my mother and the children were living with Uncle Haider and his family. When I saw them, I didn't feel any kind of relief. Everyone had lied to me from the beginning, and I had no idea who I was anymore. I was in such a bad way that nobody knew what to do with me. I understand now that I was at my lowest point, that I had fallen into a deep depression.

But then came my salvation: I was going back to Pakistan to my grandmother. She had suggested it to my mother, eager as she was to wrest us away from the clutches of my father's family and keep us with her. Basir would accompany me to Quetta in a cab and then continue his journey to Indonesia via illegal channels, where he hoped to obtain an Australian visa.

All that mattered to me was that I was going to join my sweet grandmother and my aunts who took care of me. With them, I felt loved; I felt like I belonged.

In the cab, my stepfather and I sat in hostile silence. He had already abandoned me once, and now he was leaving us altogether. After a dreary eleven-hour journey, we arrived in Quetta at dinnertime. I saw my grandmother's expression when she opened the door. I didn't know if she felt sorry for me or was distressed by my appearance. She had prepared a *shorwa*, a traditional soup, and I almost gulped down the whole pot by myself. I then polished off the meat and the bread and finally felt full.

"I can't eat any more . . . ," I said, pushing my plate away.

"That's good! Because there's nothing left," said my aunt Maha between her teeth.

The next day, my aunts took me in hand. First, Maha and Hani went with me to buy my school uniform and drove me to my old high school, the School of Light. Then a third aunt, Fatima, enrolled me at an excellent English language center. Lastly, they signed me up for their gym class. And just as I was about to devour a plate of beans with bread, my favorite dish, Maha snatched it away and slipped a plate of salad in front of me instead, stating: "You're on a diet now!"

My aunts took care of me. They made sure I ate well like they did—they were very concerned about their impeccable figures. They took me on walks and, above all, listened to me, and there were frequent fits of laughter and tears. Talking to them, I let go of my pain and lost my extra pounds. Together we sang, we painted, we drew. I lost weight quickly, I felt lighter.

They had felt frightened when I arrived, Maha confided in me one evening. Not only because I was unrecognizable, but also because of my erratic behavior—I alternated between being completely listless, hysterical, and talkative. I seemed out of control.

Maha and I had long conversations together, which would last late into the night. We talked about everything, especially my family's problems. She understood that I missed the man I saw as my father and knew that what I was going through was unfair.

I was getting better. The seven months I spent with them helped me get back on my feet, thanks to the studying, the art, the gentleness that reigned in the household, and the absence of screaming and drama. Home was now peaceful, but outside it was not. There had been another attack on the Hazara bazaar in Ali Abad, near us. It was the first time I saw Maha crying. Unlike me, she rarely let the tears take over.

But at the end of the summer, my grandmother told me I had to return to Kabul. My mother was about to give birth to her fourth child with Basir. She needed me. She was alone again. As planned, Basir had traveled to Indonesia, placing his trust in both his luck and his contacts in Kabul. He believed he would make it to Australia and promised to send for us all as soon as he got settled. In the meantime, he was in the same situation as so many other Afghans crammed into refugee camps and hoping for a way out that was unlikely to materialize. He is still there in Indonesia. No one at home believes in the Australian dream anymore.

In his absence, Mom had to raise her children without a man by her side. Life was difficult, but she was in charge. She and Basir had moved into their own house with the children while I was in Pakistan. When I returned, it was wonderful for me not to have to share her with anyone other than my brothers and my sister! However, shortly after I arrived, just as I was starting to learn music and dreaming of going to school, Uncle Haider ordered us to move back into the family compound with all its petty infighting. He, too, thought Basir's escapade was beginning to drag on for too long.

There was no way he would let his daughter-in-law and his four grandchildren live alone any longer. That would be a disgrace. Mom did as she was told with a heavy heart, even though the move solved the rent issue.

Recently I asked her how she'd felt about it all and why she didn't put up a fight. "We had nothing to eat, Homayoun was about to be born, and you were all so young. Deep down, I didn't want to go and live with them. When we did, I was filled with fear. And this fear proved itself to be justified with time. I didn't want them to touch you, but they beat you all, even the little ones. I was helpless. I was a brave young woman, and I fought to be happy . . . but they finally got to me. They succeeded in changing me. Fear became part of my life. I couldn't see any other way out."

What a thing to have to confess.

Homayoun, the last of Basir's four children, was born in December 2014, and, to this day, he still hasn't met his father. But worst of all, Basir's departure left us at the mercy of his father, Haider. The patriarch ruled over our lives now more than ever.

We had to move in with the entire family: uncles, aunts, cousins, some of them married themselves. A total of sixteen family members were spread over three floors, in a building protected by a gate that looked over a courtyard and was always closed. We had to leave our small house with its single room. Admittedly, life had been tough there, but at least it had just been us: Mom, the little ones, and me.

Haider assigned us the fourth floor, which was the least protected from both the cold and the summer heat. But it was bright and spacious, with a large kitchen, a living room, two bedrooms, and access to the roof, which provided us with a view over the whole of western Kabul. The head of the family was not doing us a favor, or looking out for us, and he certainly didn't express any joy at the idea of us moving in. But letting a woman who was part of the family and her children— one of whom was a teenager, me—live without male guardianship was out of the question. What would the neighbors say? And who knew if God might hold it against him? This way, he could keep an eye on us. For me, the situation was a disaster. I had nothing in common with my cousins, or with any member of the family, for that matter. I knew already that only trouble would follow.

On the day of my departure to Davos, I thought back to all those painful moments in my childhood. On the bus with my musician friends and Dr. Sarmast, I finally felt a sense of happiness. This was a form of revenge, triumph over adversity, for me and my mother, who was going to be proud of her daughter.

Eyes closed, fists clenched, I prayed with all my might. *Oh God, please make time stand still, here, now and forever.*

5

BAD GIRL

The European tour with Zohra really was a magical chapter in my life. The whole thing felt like a dream. Everything was going splendidly; we were buoyed by our achievements, and I was filled with a confidence I had never experienced before. The applause from the public, the interest from the journalists. Had it all gone to my head? Perhaps.

When we came back from Davos, life seemed easier at first. Negin and I were approached by several TV and radio broadcasters for interviews, including a radio station aimed at youngsters. We were asked to talk about the extraordinary journey we young Afghan girls had been on, how we'd performed for a prestigious international audience and gone on tour in Germany. They were especially curious about how we had felt during the concert and what we thought about it now that it was all over. But I also remember this one guy who hosted a morning show on TV. He was pretentious and cold, almost rude. He barely greeted me when I got to the studio. After the usual questions focusing on the concert itself, he interrogated me about my plans for the future.

"Well, I'd like to continue my education, and study political science and law at Harvard," I said, giving him my standard response.

At that point he turned to the camera arrogantly and said with disdain: "Why don't these people know their place? In my opinion, a singer should stick to singing, am I right?"

I quickly realized he had absolutely no idea what I had been doing in Davos and that I hadn't been there to sing. But apart from that man, most people—whether our close family and friends or the press—seemed to be proud of us. And so, the party continued!

At home, the family avoided me for a while. They left me alone, or rather they stopped caring what I was doing. I was confident and hopeful. I even started to believe there was going to be a "before" and "after" Davos. The incredible adventure had broadened my horizons and given me strength. Maybe anything was possible? A future that included meeting people from different backgrounds; talking to men—even strangers—as equals; responding to the media; and above all, expressing my point of view, now didn't seem so out of reach. It felt like I'd been born again. I was naive. I reveled in my memories of our tour: the cities, the concerts, the interviews.

I went back to the ANIM, where our orchestra was preparing for our winter gala with the boys from the mixed orchestra. We were feeling relaxed. We, "the Davos girls," had come back home feeling energized and motivated by the success and fame we'd gained abroad. We felt far more confident and were happy to be back at school, sharing our experiences with our classmates. The boys and older students had already had the chance to perform abroad, in Europe and even the United States. But their concerts hadn't attracted as much attention as ours. Fortunately, they didn't seem bitter or jealous about it in the slightest, and everyone was in good spirits as we rehearsed together.

I was finally reunited with my dear friends Samir, Samim, and Shiraz. Regardless of the disapproving looks, we would hug each other when we got to school in the morning. We were always messing around, joking, and chatting about everything under the sun. This was very rare in Afghanistan. Only at the ANIM, where the principles of diversity, liberty, and equality reigned, could such a friendship group exist. Anywhere else, it would have been unthinkable. Our bond was stronger than ever. Our shared sense of humor both united us and saved us from the heavy burdens of our society. One of us needed only to wink at the others for them to catch on. Our friendship was free of prejudice. Gender and ethnicity weren't important to us, and they treated me like one of them. Now more than ever, we shared the same dreams: to support our families and lead happy, fulfilling lives.

Even now, when I mention this unique friendship, it amazes my female Afghan friends, who ask, "But how is that possible?" Many of them have reached adulthood without having so much as shaken a boy's hand!

Shiraz, who played the clarinet and was a head taller than the rest of us, had a sharp sense of humor and gave us all nicknames. Mine was Pochoq, which literally translates as "small nose." This common insult was frequently aimed at the Hazaras, but Shiraz used it affectionately: "Zarifa, if I was forced to choose between all the Pashtuns in the world and you, I'd pick you. I swear. That's how much I like you," he once told me.

Samim was given the nickname Bini, which also means "nose," but in his case it was because he had the longest nose in the whole class! During religious studies, Shiraz pretended to ask our teacher with the utmost seriousness: "Sir, when we pray, is it necessary for our foreheads to touch the floor?"

"Yes, absolutely. Your forehead must touch the prayer mat," replied our teacher.

"But look at Samim, and that long nose of his—it must be difficult for him, right?" he quipped.

The entire class burst out laughing. Jokes like these were a daily occurrence.

We spent most of our days together, chatting, singing, playing, talking about everything and nothing. Those three boys were the best friends I'd ever had in Afghanistan. We were always there for one another. And music was the thing that had brought us all together right from the start. We were friends and musicians before being girls or boys. Most of all, their unwavering loyalty had allowed me to rid myself of the idea—instilled in me since childhood—that a girl is worth less than a boy. Not only was I worth as much as them, but sometimes, I proved myself even smarter. They will back me up on this, I know.

For my mother, all of this was obviously unacceptable. In her eyes, I seemed incapable of doing anything right or behaving like everyone else—and that included my choice of friends. Hanging out with boys was already unthinkable, but to make things worse, we were all of different ethnicities: Shiraz was Pashtun, Samim was Tajik, and Samir was Uzbek and Tajik. This had never been an issue for us, but it was for Mom. However, she would eventually change her mind when she met them at the ANIM. She even admitted they were very nice and respectful, before adding that I shouldn't see them outside of school or have my picture taken with them.

Once again, only the progressive and caring environment of the music school could allow such a friendship to flourish. And now we would be performing together very soon, though this time, unfortunately, it would be in front of a much smaller audience than the one Zohra performed for at Davos. For security reasons, and to avoid attracting the attention of extremist groups, the ANIM never publicized their local performances. There was a perpetual fear of terror attacks.

In addition to my studies, I taught English in a small language school for two hours per day. I had two classes of children who loved me, and I loved them. I had so often had to do things alone, including learning English from scratch, that it was a real pleasure to teach others and encourage the pupils in their studies, like I did with my brother Ali and my little sister, Najla. I earned four thousand afghanis per month (less than sixty dollars), and this was a real help to the family.

It had been almost three years since I returned from Quetta, and Basir remained stuck in Indonesia; he still seemed to believe he could get a visa—or at least he pretended to believe it. Mom had five children now and had to manage everything on her own. I had become the family's sole source of income beyond our hundred-dollar allowance from Haider. My contribution was essential for the provision of our daily needs and, most importantly, for paying my brothers' and sister's school fees. From the outside, all seemed well. But the reality was quite different.

Deep down, I was uneasy. The video of my interview with *USA Today* had been circulating on the internet for the past couple of weeks, and had generated a lot of comments, both positive and negative. The kindest comments really did me good:

"That's what feminism looks like!" wrote one girl.

"Strong and well-educated girls/women are the future!" gushed another. One said, "I've always loved 'bad girls'!"

On the other hand, the worst comments were caustic, disapproving, and sanctimonious.

"No good Muslim would talk like that," insisted one anonymous viewer who said they were "proud to be a good Muslim," and who was, as often happens, confusing religious practices with Afghan traditions.

Even more disappointingly, another wrote: "My father lets me go to school and do whatever I want and that doesn't make me a 'bad girl.'" Basically, she was undermining everything I had said, without considering that she obviously came from an extremely privileged background that represented only a tiny portion of the population, even in Kabul.

Some critics suspected I wanted pity or attention. Others accused me of "spreading Western propaganda" by criticizing our society and way of life or seemed to think I was bitter in some way, as in the case of comments like: "Looks like *someone's* visa was rejected . . . nice try, idiot!"

Openly declaring—to a foreign reporter, no less—that I was a "bad girl" because I wanted to study, travel, and do what I loved had been a real provocation. I knew that, and I knew, too, that this could cause trouble. I was conscious of the risks this situation posed and was being even more careful. When I walked around the city by myself now, I often wore a mask that covered the bottom half of my face, so I wouldn't be recognized.

But I wasn't the only one who was afraid. There had been numerous acid attacks targeting girls in Kabul, and all of us in the Zohra Orchestra knew we could be the next victims. How to protect ourselves from these attacks, the fear of being burnt, disfigured . . . it's all we talked about. We were scared of retaliation after our European tour. And, evidently, we fed off each other in our fear.

Several weeks after Davos, my friend Marjan and I were walking not far from the ANIM. It's located in a student district with various schools and institutes, and the neighborhood is a safe one—safer than mine—so I felt secure there normally. Before we reached the school, four boys approached us, elbowing each other and staring.

"Hey, look! It's the girls from the orchestra!"

They must have been around twenty-two or twenty-three years old. I wasn't wearing my mask, and it was extremely unpleasant to be recognized on the street. Petrified, we continued to walk, holding each other a bit more tightly. Without looking at me, Marjan whispered: "If they attack us, turn your head away as fast as possible. That way, the acid will hit your shoulder and not your face. Protecting your face is the most important thing."

Suddenly, two of them separated from the group, heightening our panic. We immediately thought: *This is it. They've gone to get the acid.* We threw ourselves into a taxi that was passing by at just the right moment! The poor boys were probably harmless. In truth, I was constantly terrified of attacks back then.

I was harassed on the street more and more often. Men didn't necessarily recognize me as "Zarifa, the orchestra conductor," but my appearance and clothes bothered them: my dresses, my leggings, my tennis shoes, my headscarf sitting loosely on my hair. Even though we were in Kabul, the war and the influx of people from the provinces, who had been displaced by the violence, were causing old-fashioned attitudes and mentalities to be increasingly reinforced. When I look at photographs from Kabul taken thirty or forty years ago, I see girls' bare heads and skirts that ended at the knees. That would be unthinkable these days. It feels like our society is narrowing, like hearts and minds are locking down rather than opening up. The worse the situation in the country gets, the more the mindset of the population stiffens, tenses, becomes inflexible. War truly destroys everything. I learned this while growing up in Kabul: the unfair war had taken so much away from us.

And if progress was just a memory now, I wondered, what was going to happen to my little sister, Najla, who aspired to be a track star? Was it possible that things could get even worse?

Lively and mischievous, with curly brown hair, Najla is, at the time I write this, a clever twelve-year-old who enjoys her food. She dreams of competing in a stadium, running until she is out of breath, free, without worrying about what anyone will say. She loves school and gets good grades, but her ambitions lie elsewhere. In her dreams she is on the podium, having won the hundred-meter sprint, standing with a gold medal around her neck—an Olympic champion!—as the Afghan national anthem plays in the background through the speakers.

I wanted to do everything in my power to protect her and support her in her ambitions. I knew she got tired, sometimes, of the tensions and drama I caused in the family. I knew she got frustrated when our mother would take Ali, our oldest brother, to eat kebabs in a restaurant and leave us girls at home to take care of the younger ones. In Kabul, when there wasn't enough money to buy meat for everyone, it was reserved for the boys, who needed to grow up big and strong. My mother was perfectly aware of this way of thinking and accepted it. But Najla, determined to escape this fate assigned to her by the chance of gender, always took it hard.

One day Najla and I were in our neighborhood, walking home together, and a man who was around thirty years old charged at me, yelling that he could see my hair—I was wearing my headscarf, but I had purposefully let it slip back. He also scolded me for the knee-length dress I was wearing over my leggings. He used a vulgar, sexually charged word and accused me of being indecent. Najla was shocked. I tried to calm her down.

"Don't worry. That guy is crazy. Don't look at him."

"But what does he want? Why is he insulting you? He doesn't *look* crazy . . ."

Najla is rational. She likes things to mean something, to make sense. But how could I explain to her that this guy had screamed obscenities at me just because of the way I wore my headscarf? Men seem to feel like they can do anything they want in this society. They believe they have the right to judge women, criticize us, and even insult us. All we can do is keep our mouths shut and walk away. What other choice do we have? I grabbed my sister's hand and ran.

It was around this time that the "bad girl" video, having made the rounds on the internet, reached our household. My dear cousins, who'd heard about it from their friends, ratted me out and showed it to everyone in the family. Thankfully, I had kept my headscarf on during all of my interviews and throughout the whole tour—thank you, Mom! You could only see my bangs, combed to one side. I had taken great pains not to provoke anyone with my appearance, not wanting to provide my critics with further ammunition. But this interview revealed the truth to my family. I hadn't, in fact, gone to Davos as Zohra's translator or as only a spokeswoman. I had gone as a musician, as a conductor.

The Uncles and their wives, and Haider's wife, in particular, immediately kicked up a fuss. It was the perfect opportunity to criticize me. All the women of the family—aunts, cousins, wives, nieces—got together to watch the video and give a running commentary.

That night, when I arrived home, they were all sitting together on *toshaks* spread around the living room that was on the floor below ours. Mom silently signaled for me to go up to our floor without being seen. But Uncle Haider called me down, and I had to obey him. I felt like I was appearing before a tribunal; I was the defendant, and I didn't have a lawyer.

"So, you're all over social media now?! Everyone has seen you and knows you are a musician. You've brought shame upon this family."

"Don't worry, Uncle. I will finish this school year, and then I will go abroad. I want to study law at an American university. You'll see, you'll be proud of me."

I tried to remain poised, respectful, calm, and, above all, to act naturally—even if, in his eyes, there was nothing natural about a girl who played the viola, traveled abroad alone, wanted to study in another country, and was also part of his family. I tried to think of what I could say in my defense. It was only then that I understood that he wasn't only concerned about my face being on the internet. He hadn't known that I was a musician, much less a conductor, at all.

This interview clip had come as a revelation for him, a total and utter shock. The family had thought that all I'd been doing was going to school, period. There had never been any talk of me attending music school, even after I went to Davos.

Up until that point, I'd been unaware that Mom had lied to cover for me when I left, saying I was only traveling as an interpreter. When she had passed on my family's congratulations to me during the tour, my uncle hadn't seen our concerts; he'd seen only the pictures of me at Zohra's press conference in Davos. Since he didn't speak English, he hadn't understood what I was saying. But he had seen me on stage—wearing my headscarf—talking to an attentive international audience, and this had been a source of pride for him.

After my return, I had deliberately spoken vaguely when asked about the orchestra's adventures and performances. I avoided the family as much as I could. I knew, or rather I suspected, that when they got together, they insulted me in front of my mother. They even made disparaging remarks about me to our neighbors and relatives, saying, "She went abroad alone. She spends time with *men*," and now they would add: "On top of everything, she plays *music*."

Mom was becoming more and more anxious and depressed. Everyone now knew her daughter was a musician and performed in an orchestra. "Who will marry you now? Nobody will want anything to do with you!"

I was sullied. Untouchable. In Afghanistan, when a man wants to get married, the reputation of his future wife is scrutinized, her morals and past investigated in full. Her life must be a clean slate. The perfect girl has no relationships with boys, has no pictures or videos posted on Facebook, wears a headscarf that is always tightly wrapped, and is in good health. Her family, too, must be irreproachable. Everything is double-checked, analyzed, and judged by the suitor's relatives. The girl needs to be inoffensive and pure. She must have the right profile, make no mistakes, be faultless.

One day, as I was sitting in the back of a minibus in Kabul with other girls, I heard a young man in the front explain to his friend on the phone why he had decided to call off his engagement.

"It's not going to be possible," he argued. "I saw a picture of her smoking. I can't marry a girl who's been seen smoking!"

He wouldn't calm down. Yet, he admitted the girl suited him otherwise. The person on the other end of the line seemed to agree with his conclusion. Although none of this stopped him from lighting a cigarette of his own as soon as he got off the bus. Because boys can do whatever they like. They can date girls, drink, smoke, travel, and nobody will ever think to check their background or ask them to disclose if they have indulged in any of these shenanigans, or really hold it against them if they have.

In that context, where, to put it simply, a girl is always in the wrong and the men are always right, my dreams and my ambitions indeed made me a "bad girl." I studied. I was a musician. I had traveled without a chaperone to the United States, Turkey, and Europe. I worked with boys. All of which is to say, I didn't exactly tick the right boxes. Of course, certain girls, like my friend Negin, are supported by their parents or sometimes by an elder brother, and so have the opportunity to study and work even after they get married.

I knew a cheerful, straightforward man from my neighborhood who made kites. With the help of his children, he skillfully cut up pieces of colorful tissue paper and, by the dim light of a hurricane lamp, stuck them onto a frame of thin curved sticks. He sold the results for a couple of pennies apiece up on Wazir Akbar Khan hill, where children went in the winter, especially on Fridays, to fly kites. He very nearly earned a living from this—although to do so he still needed to sell an awful lot of kites. But he was determined to see his eldest daughter and, later, her younger sisters, go to university. He held tightly on to this dream with great humility. Similarly, Negin's father would always come to watch his daughter perform with Zohra in Kabul. But such behavior remains rare. The thinking goes: What good does it do to educate girls if they are just going to stay at home anyway?

In my family, all the wives, aunts, cousins, and even their female neighbors were incredibly proud when their daughters stayed at home full-time to await a husband, and so they were horrified by my behavior. They would tell my mother over and over again that nobody would want to marry a girl like me. *A girl like me . . .*

Their primary concern, their main preoccupation, was marrying off their daughters. An unmarried girl presents a risk for the family, the risk of dishonor. She mustn't fall in love with the wrong boy, or even think about running away with him, much less fall pregnant. One of my aunts from the Uncles' side of the family, the most toxic couple in the house, was gratified by her own self-imposed alienation from the world. She was thrilled about it even: "I never leave the house without my husband. I won't go anywhere without him."

It was exasperating. Her husband kept her on a tight leash, and she was proud of it!

Conversely, my emancipation was shameful to them. The fact that I lived as I did, with relative freedom, meant I was "unsellable" on the marriage market. My mother was finding the situation more and more difficult to handle. She didn't know how to stand up for herself, having been relegated to the role of victim ever since the end of her childhood. One day she cracked under the pressure of their constant criticism and forbade me from going to the ANIM anymore.

Depriving me of the ANIM meant depriving me of music, and also of an education. I was almost nineteen years old and was completing my last year of high school. Our successive house moves and the to and fro between Afghanistan and Pakistan had meant I had some catching up to do. I knew that I would have graduated a long time ago if I had been living abroad. I was already falling behind. So, this news devastated me. I pleaded, cried, begged, and argued: "Not now! Not when I'm so close to the end! How will I get to university if I haven't finished high school?

"Mom, I beg you. Ignore the gossip. Don't worry. You'll see. One day I'll meet someone worthy. A good husband for me and a good son-in-law for you."

But there was nothing I could do about it. In her eyes, we were fighting a losing battle.

"It's impossible, Zarifa. You live in Afghanistan, and in our society that just won't happen. You're already getting old to marry. If we wait any longer, nobody will want you."

I tried to convince her every night, tried to comfort her and make her laugh, too. Where was that proud Anis Gul who had stood up to the rich girls in her village?

"Forget all these women who want to belittle me, Mom. You know what? I wouldn't want their sons for anything in the world. They are not worthy. They don't deserve me. They can keep them!"

Unfortunately—and this is something I've noticed often—it's frequently the women themselves who create trouble for other women. This is true of the wider community, not just within my family; it is not common for women in Afghanistan to support one another. I see it at work and in my day-to-day life; women constantly bad-mouthing others and judging those who stand out. It's painful to admit, but it's the truth. This gossiping and belittling of each other arises from their ignorance. They have been kept away from school and books their entire lives. If they understood the good that could come from standing up for one another, girls' lives in Afghanistan would be very different.

We are in desperate need of solidarity. If a woman wants to be independent or goes against the grain, she is hunted down by the rest of the pack. This does us so much more harm than good in our patriarchal society. Men intuitively sense this and take advantage. Because of this, it can feel more important for girls and women to comply with men's expectations than to reach out to their fellow women.

I'm lucky enough to have met some remarkable people in my home country. A handful of men who believed in me and supported me in my projects and aspirations. But I was also helped by strong, loyal women like my American viola teacher, Jennifer Moberg, whom I called "Miss Jennifer," and, of course, my aunt Maha, whose elegance, imagination, good taste, and artistic talents I've always envied.

In contrast, at home—or more accurately, in our family building—the atmosphere was becoming more and more oppressive, fed by jealousy, resentment, and hate. The video had really left its mark. Mom was struggling more than ever to live with the consequences of this taboo behavior. She told me a mullah had threatened us. On the street, he had shoved a piece of paper in her face claiming that music was haram: "It's demonic! It's a sin!"

"He told me he'd issued a fatwa against you. Something bad is going to happen to you, Zarifa."

She was terrified. She was considering going to the police, but she didn't trust them, either. Would a policeman ever take a woman's side against a mullah? And anyway, our police force is totally corrupt. I've heard many stories about women who have gone to report domestic abuse to the police, only to be taken back home to their husbands. Or rape victims who were given a lecture about their morals, forced to take a virginity test, or even sexually assaulted again.

It was around this time when Bilal, Ahmad's younger brother—my half brother—called me from the United States, where he lived. He was one of the few members of the family who had always been kind to me, and we had kept in touch. After graduating with a diploma in engineering, he had worked at the American military base in Jalalabad in the east, which had allowed him to get an immigrant visa relatively easily and leave Afghanistan for good. He had settled in California. When he'd found out I was first going to Yale for the summer program and, a couple months later, on the orchestra's European tour, he had encouraged me to seize the opportunity to run away. He now thought that by ignoring his advice, I had dug my own grave.

"I told you not to go back to Kabul. I told you to stay here when you came for your program. But you didn't listen. You were so happy to have played a song when you went to Europe."

Yes, he really did call what we did "a song"!

"Look at you now," he said. "No one cares about all that. Nobody respects you."

"But what did you expect, Bilal?" I thundered. "That I'd go it alone, become an illegal, have no prospects beyond becoming a cleaning lady? So many people in Kabul told me the same thing: stay in the United States, make the most of it! But what would my future have been? I want to study. I want to be someone, feel respected and useful. I don't want to live abroad as an undocumented refugee. I want to change things in Afghanistan." There was something inside me that kept telling me, *There are many things that you must do for Afghanistan, Zarifa.* I didn't know what those things were, or what I might ever have the power to do. But I believed that I would certainly do something. No one else thought it was possible. Even my dear aunt Maha used to make fun of me for dreaming that I could do something for my country.

He hung up, almost angry at me. But I knew what I was talking about. Dr. Sarmast had warned his students, telling us about his own experiences as a legal, not even illegal, refugee in Australia, the country that had given him political asylum in 1994.

"When I got there, I couldn't speak a word of English. My diplomas were worthless, they weren't recognized. I had to restart my studies and pass my exams all over again and work at the same time. I accepted lots of small jobs to earn enough to support my family; I was a barman and a mover, among other things."

Dr. Sarmast, the musician and future founder of the ANIM, moving other peoples' furniture?! His story most likely dissuaded a lot of us from running away, because very few ANIM musicians have ever taken advantage of a foreign tour to disappear. Those who have, including a few girls, were escaping violence or a forced marriage.

I could have done the same, but I'd never wanted to. My dreams were not of escape but of changing things for my country.

Uncle Haider provided me with another reason for regret. He came to find me one evening while I was doing the laundry. I can still see myself so clearly, in my leggings and shirt, sleeves rolled up and hair tied back, no headscarf. I wasn't exactly formally attired. He announced, point-blank: "Zarifa, somebody is here to ask for your hand in marriage."

The man's name was Hassib. Mom was very nervous. He was a member of her family, and she needed things to work out. She didn't want the slightest whiff of scandal reaching her village.

"Oh, Zarifa! Nobody can see you dressed like that! Go get changed quickly," she whispered in a panic.

Come on, what's happening here? You really want to marry me off? The threat of such a thing happening was no longer hypothetical. It was sitting on the living room cushions. The boy and his father had traveled from Ghazni. For the first time, a potential suitor was actually here, in the flesh.

I refused to meet him. According to Mom, who complimented him lavishly, he was a self-taught mechanic who was around twenty-seven or twenty-eight years old. He lived two hours away in a rural and conservative area southeast of Kabul—one that has since been taken over by the Taliban. This was where they wanted to send me?!

Everyone around me seemed genuinely hopeful that I would go with him, settle in his village, and stay locked in his house, having children and doing chores for the rest of my life. The worst part was my mother seemed delighted at the prospect, which only reinforced my despair and sense of abandonment. As for the Uncles, they clearly wanted to get rid of me and send me to a backwater as far away as possible; they wanted me to stop going to school, and to give up on my studies and ambitions.

I refused outright. I stood my ground. I was fuming inside and terrified.

Uncle Haider was furious. After that, and after finding out that Basir had sent us some money once or twice, he decided not to help us financially anymore. He began by withholding the several afghanis he normally gave my mother for my brothers' and sister's school bus fees, just to make life more difficult for us. He also hoped to turn my siblings against me by making me appear to be responsible for their suffering.

Mom would have liked for me to agree to this marriage and make her life easier. She didn't know what to do with me anymore. This feeling wasn't new, and she once again called my grandmother in Pakistan to ask for advice. The threats, the pressure from the Uncles, the mullah, and the fatwa all terrified her.

"It's too risky here for Zarifa," my mother said of life in Afghanistan. "And since it's going so badly with the family, maybe it's best if she does get married."

She was, despite everything, fairly happy at the prospect of being able to use this marriage proposal—the first one her rebel child had gotten—to assert herself with the mothers-in-law, sisters-in-law, and cousins. If her daughter got married, she, too, would be granted a better social status; she would be a young mother-in-law and, soon enough, a young grandmother. But, on the other end of the line, her own mother reacted at once.

"Out of the question! Don't do it!" my grandmother almost shouted.

She was still grieving the marriage she had forced upon her daughter. My grandmother had never forgiven herself for abandoning her beautiful Anis Gul to her new husband and moving so far away from her. My grandparents immediately suggested an alternative.

"Come to Pakistan. Bring the children and stay here until your husband gets his Australian visa. The situation in Afghanistan is getting worse by the day anyway."

For me, the proposed move was a catastrophe. On the one hand, I was scared of the Uncles and dreaded a forced marriage—who would come to my aid? I had no father and now not even a stepfather.

On the other hand, leaving Kabul meant leaving the ANIM, giving up my music and my studies. I was so close to graduating from high school: my first step toward university. I still paid rapt attention to Michelle Obama's every word and wanted, above all else, to continue my education. "Nothing should distract girls from their ambitions," I could hear her insisting. But Mom had made her decision. She wanted to leave, to be with her mother and sisters again, and was determined to keep us safe; she was too vulnerable without a husband.

And once again, not wanting to upset her—although I didn't really have the choice anyway—I did my part. I started to get the money together for the trip. I borrowed here and there from my friends, from my teachers, and so on. I ended up with three hundred dollars, enough for us to leave for Quetta by cab.

The Uncles alerted Basir, who was still in Indonesia.

"Your family wants to leave, but where will they go? How will they sustain themselves? We won't be giving them a cent," warned Haider, taking advantage of his son's sense of honor and authority.

It worked. That very evening, Basir called Mom. "If you really want to leave, go ahead, and take your daughter with you," he said, raising his voice. "But don't touch my children."

"My children"! He had never even met the youngest.

Mom crumbled. She couldn't do it. She couldn't stand up to her husband, even if there were thousands of miles separating them. For me, this was a blow to the heart; betrayal had dealt me a mean uppercut. Basir had said: "*Your* daughter. *My* children." This man who once made no distinction between me and his children, who had always been a father figure, had rejected me again. That night, something also broke inside Mom. Basir, her husband, had just thrown her past in her face. I was once again the source of her misery.

"Get out of my sight!" she screamed, full of rage. "Just disappear!"

I lay down on the rooftop and looked up at the sky. Davos's heroine, lost under the stars. The same girl who had been so applauded three months earlier was now a social pariah. I couldn't sleep; neither could I cry.

I called my dear friend Samir, my soulmate from the ANIM, and asked him to meet me in Shar-e-Naw, the "new district" of shops and cafés. There I cried as I told him all about the drama with my stepfather, the aborted attempt to move to Pakistan, and the dead end at which I now found myself. Samir took care of everything that day. I didn't want to leave all alone in a taxi, so he bought me a plane ticket to Islamabad.

"I know that someday I'll be the one borrowing money from you," he said, smiling to put me at ease.

Before I left home, I took a hundred dollars from the money I had saved up for our move and left two hundred for my mother.

While Samir arranged everything for me, I went to the ANIM and asked to see Dr. Sarmast. I wanted to explain to him why I couldn't continue my music studies. He was preoccupied with a family problem himself and manifestly didn't understand why I was leaving. He thought I had decided on a whim, that my head had been turned by the allure of living abroad, and that I saw Pakistan as a springboard, my first step to the West. His reaction saddened me, but I had neither the time nor the strength to try to explain myself more fully.

I took the flight to Islamabad and then another to Quetta, this one paid for by Maha. All I had in terms of luggage was a small backpack—the one we had been given in Davos—which contained my most precious possessions: a couple of notebooks and my diaries. My viola belonged to the ANIM, and so, of course, I had to leave it behind. I felt like I had lost everything at once: my instrument, my school, my music, my father, even the rest of my family. Once again, I had been cut out of the photo, erased from the story. Basir's harsh words, filled with hate, had snatched away everything I had fought so hard to achieve. I felt a profound sense of injustice, which soon turned to resentment.

Here I was, being dragged back into the past, when all I had ever wanted was to look to the future.

6

IN TALIBAN TERRITORY

I arrived in Quetta at dawn. In Islamabad, a Pakistani friend I'd met at Yale had taken me out for brunch before driving me back to the airport. I had kept my departure and especially my travel details a secret from almost everyone. Nobody apart from my aunt Maha knew I was coming. She hadn't wanted to worry my grandmother, so she hadn't told her I was traveling there on my own, and I certainly didn't want to reveal my real reasons for leaving and the details of my latest fight with my mother and stepfather. So Maha was the only one who actually knew what was happening. When I got off the plane, she was waiting for me. Seeing her again was an enormous comfort.

My grandparents had moved since I last visited. They had sold their big house, and my grandfather had gone to work in Australia—yes, *he* had been able to get a visa. My grandmother and aunts were now living on the ground floor of a more modest house. A corridor led from the bright blue front door to a living room, two bedrooms, and a small kitchen. The owner lived on the floor above. Nevertheless, I noticed most of the furniture and carpets were the same as before, and the place was kept as shiny, clean, and cozy as their previous home.

Once she had gotten over her shock, my grandmother quickly became suspicious: "Why didn't you tell us anything? Zarifa, your mother knows you're with us, right?" she asked, looking at me severely.

"Of course she knows." She did know. But she had encouraged me to go, and Basir had come between me and my mother and siblings, and so I hadn't wanted to stay in their house any longer. I could have remained in Afghanistan if I'd had their support. I'd done it before. But I was hurt by Basir's and my mother's treatment of me, and I didn't feel like their home was my home anymore.

I told my grandmother why I had run away, and she listened to me without uttering a word. When it came to Mom and men, it certainly seemed that things were still complicated.

I was extremely close to Maha. My young aunt was willful and headstrong and was studying art at the time. I admired her elegance, her joyfulness, and her free spirit. She had a style unique to her, original and imaginative. And above all, she knew how to listen to me and understood my loneliness.

My grandparents were wonderful, too. They had always been there for me and were loving, generous, and forgiving. They were demanding but also indulgent. At the time, my grandfather was working on a farm in Australia, near Sydney. He spoiled me and gave me an iPhone—it was my first smartphone! I couldn't believe it. I think that pleasing me and showing he cared were particularly important to him. Once again, my grandparents, who had married their daughter off so young, proved they would stop at nothing to prevent the same sad story from happening again all these years later, like a family curse.

Despite all this, I felt like I was going around in circles. I had left everything behind: the music school, my friends, my mother, my brothers, and my sister. What was I going to do with my life? I saw no future for myself, and I feared that the curse of being born a girl would always catch up with me. Was I going to have to eventually fall in line? Forever give up my studies? My chance at independence, success, happiness? I'd had only a taste of these things, and I knew that I wanted more of them. But it seemed that my chances to gain them were disappearing. I had lost the "bad girl" somewhere along the way; she remained a prisoner in Kabul. After the initial joy of my reunion with my mother's family had passed, I once again felt discouraged. I was in a dark place, but this was unlike my last trip to Pakistan. I'd gotten a glimpse of what life had to offer since then. And I was acutely aware of all that there was for me to lose.

One weary evening, I told Maha, "I'm so sick of this life."

Maha pounced. "Well, what is it you want to do, then? Give up? Okay, give up. After all, it's your life, right? We can find you a nice boy so you can get married and let your husband take care of you. Do you want to go back to Kabul, or should we start looking here?"

Her anger got to me. Maha the artist, who always looked impeccable, her long hair tied up with a flower to frame her thin face, delicately made up. Maha, who had fought to study, and who took endless care of me, encouraging me to paint, draw, dance, and sing with her. I couldn't let her down.

The most urgent task was to find a school that would let me study in Farsi and obtain my Afghan high school diploma so that all my academic work up to that point wouldn't go to waste—especially since I had already been forced to interrupt my music lessons. After much effort and many tests, I was finally accepted at the Ferdawsi High School. Once I got there, I decided to keep the fact I was a musician to myself. I'm not quite sure why. I was probably afraid of attracting more trouble. I preferred to fade into the background. However, after just three days there, one of the two girls who sat next to me showed up for class acting very excited.

"You're the girl from that video, right? The one about music?"

I confirmed it. Yes, that was me—I was the "bad girl."

She immediately told her friend, and both of them started bombarding me with questions. One of them even wanted to go to Kabul to join the ANIM and study there. I became her mentor and I loved it! She was fortunate enough to be fully supported by her parents, and her main challenge in life was finding how to make the most of this opportunity. So, I did everything I could to motivate her. She didn't go in the end; she quickly became distracted by whatever next new thing drew her attention away.

At school, I happily resumed my English lessons. That language was my path to the future. It had led me to the Turkish coast, to Yale, and then to the podium in Davos.

Despite my family's limited resources, I had managed to teach myself, after learning the basics during the first years of middle school in Quetta. When we'd returned to Kabul—well before I went to the ANIM, where English classes were mandatory—I had convinced a female friend of mine who was taking lessons to share her class notes with me. In the evening, I would run to her house and copy things down and would then go off and learn them. Later on, accessing the internet—usually at the ANIM—helped with my English a lot, especially watching American TV and Michelle Obama's speeches.

At first, I would try to find videos of her speeches in the original English with subtitles to improve my vocabulary. *Michelle*, needless to say, ended up providing me not just with a better grasp of her mother tongue but also a passion for school and my studies. I wonder if one day the former first lady will find out how she helped a young Afghan girl learn the language of Shakespeare.

Now that I was back in Quetta, I also tried to find music classes, but I no longer had an instrument, and I couldn't find a viola teacher. However, I got lucky, once again, when two guardian angels crossed my path. Alarmed by my depressing Facebook posts, an old teacher of mine from the ANIM, Chris Stone—who had since gone back to Australia—called on several occasions to encourage me. He persisted and found the right words to motivate me. His calls and my aunts' unwavering affection convinced me not to give up, inspiring me to get back up and fight.

It was at that point that I received a big parcel that had been carefully wrapped in cardboard and bubble wrap. My grandparents and I were eating lunch when Maha brought it to me. My heart was thumping as I read the sender's address: "Northampton, United Kingdom." The sender was Dan, my friend Dan! Dan Blackwell was an English musician and documentary maker who had come to visit Zohra at the ANIM.

I immediately felt sure it was a viola, and I began to scream with joy. I hugged Maha so tight. I ripped open the package while my aunt looked on, amused. I simply couldn't believe it. A viola! It was missing a couple of strings and a tuning peg, but that was nothing that couldn't be fixed.

The instrument was a godsend. It was worth more to me than all the riches in the world put together. As I held it up against me, my happiness knew no bounds. This may sound exaggerated, but it felt like I had been reunited with an old friend who, placing their hand on my shoulder, said: "Don't worry. Everything is going to be okay." Thank you, Dan.

Dan had come to the ANIM shortly before I left Kabul. He had seen the "bad girl" video, read the press articles, and listened to extracts of Zohra's concert in Davos. He was so interested in our unusual story that he'd come to Kabul to see us in person.

Dan led the project 4bar Collective, which provided a unique and free platform for musicians and artists around the world. He traveled all over to record musicians and showcase their talent; his aim in doing so was also to promote peace, to encourage people to better understand one another, and to overcome divides and fight against extremism. For example, he had made a film about an orchestra composed of Israelis and Palestinians who were united by a shared passion for music. After discovering Zohra on the internet, he thought our story was "so inspiring," in his words, that he composed a song for us: "Sister." He released it on Facebook with an open letter that introduced Zohra to readers of the post. He then contacted Dr. Sarmast, who immediately invited him to come meet us. I had also replied to his post, and we'd started chatting online. We'd had lengthy exchanges about music and the obstacles musicians in Afghanistan faced.

"Six months later, I was on the plane to Kabul to record a piece with Zohra's musicians. I wanted to pay tribute to them and acknowledge all they had done for women's rights. That trip became a thirty-minute documentary about the orchestra," recalled Dan.

I remember that when he arrived in Afghanistan, I was the one who guided his driver to the ANIM over the phone. Dan didn't know I was planning to leave soon for Quetta and that I was actually calling him from home. Once he got to the school, he was worried when he saw I wasn't there, and even more concerned when no one could tell him why. At the time, Mom had just forbidden me from going to the ANIM, and I had disappeared without any explanation.

Dan called my home that night to see how I was doing. He didn't give up until he'd spoken to me, not understanding that his calls made my mother even more suspicious about what I was up to. I was forced to tell him what was happening and that, much to my regret, I was about to leave Kabul. He nonetheless managed to convince me to meet him at school the next day, and we sat down and had a long talk. That day he recorded an extensive interview with me during which I opened up to him, telling him how unbearable the thought of leaving the Zohra Orchestra was to me.

When I watch this video now, I think I look tired and pale, with my pink headscarf tied around my neck and my drawn features. I was on the verge of tears. Dan and I talked about everything together. We immediately grew very close, like old friends, two souls who had found each other despite the age difference. Facing him, with his light-colored eyes and tattoos, I felt like I was in the presence of a rock star! Once again, music had brought another person and me together. Dan and I both believed music was more than just entertainment; it was a bridge between people, a universal language as well as a tool for peace.

That day, I said goodbye to my friends at the ANIM and confessed to Dan that, on top of having to leave, what really broke my heart was having to abandon my viola. Back in the UK, Dan quickly proceeded to edit a selection of extracts from my interview and released them online to launch a fund to buy me a new viola. He had told me about this, but I hadn't believed it would really happen. I thought he was just trying to make me feel better. And yet, what he'd said was true. I would find out only much later via a friend that he had, in fact, paid for my viola out of his own pocket before the money came in, reimbursing himself after the donations arrived. "Don't worry," he joked when I told him I'd found out about this. "We musicians are used to being broke!"

And that's how I got my viola.

By that point, it was already the beginning of December. I had been in Quetta for eight months and I was getting nowhere. But I was trying as hard as I could to set my life back on track and doing everything I could think of to move in the right direction: I continued going to school and at the same time kept a lookout for a job or an opportunity to study abroad, such as working as an au pair or a tutor. Turning this unforeseen setback into a fresh start would be a sweet form of revenge. I consulted ads online and got in touch with anyone and everyone I could think of to make new contacts and obtain letters of recommendation. All of it to no avail. It was too difficult for a potential American or European employer to obtain a visa for an Afghan au pair, much less one who had no official qualifications.

It was then that my mother asked me to come back to Kabul. The last time that had happened, she'd been about to give birth. This time, however, she explained to my grandmother that she was sick and tired. She needed me at home. She couldn't manage without me, alone with the children—even if Ali was almost fourteen and Najla, thirteen. Once again, she was asking me to give up the life I had built for myself and come back.

But come back and do what? Stay at home and clean up after everyone? I wasn't enthusiastic about this latest development, and Maha was downright angry over it. She thought her sister was being selfish. Obviously, the prospect of being imprisoned again within the putrid atmosphere of the family compound, surrounded by the family's suffocating gossip and maliciousness, weighed heavily on me. Yet running away to Pakistan had forced me to abandon my music, the ANIM, and many of my life goals. I missed Zohra and conducting. I had little chance of picking up the baton again in Pakistan, and no hope of getting into university there. All this, less than a year after the triumph of Davos.

Going back wasn't an attractive prospect, but I had nothing concrete or stimulating keeping me in Quetta. After all, though I had been stung by my stepfather's cruel words, he'd spoken the plain and simple truth: I wasn't his daughter. And besides, my grandmother and Aunt Maha had just gotten their visas for Australia. They planned to leave and join my grandfather in a couple of months. And despite my pleas for them to take me with them, they were unable to do so.

I only had one option. I had to go back the way I had come, had to go back to Afghanistan. It was my country, and at least for the moment, that was where my future lay. I didn't know what to expect: a forced marriage, a fresh kick in the teeth from my family, scorn from my community. I didn't know what to hope for. I dreaded returning to a world constrained by bitterness and sadness, and I dreaded the possibility that I might have to witness Zohra's triumphs at a distance, achieved without me. Could I really expect to earn back my place in the orchestra after so many months away? I also knew I would have to find enough work to be able to help Mom and the four children financially. On top of everything else, conditions in Afghanistan had deteriorated even further—the country was experiencing attacks and bloodshed almost every day.

Following a series of particularly deadly explosions, Kabul was now considered to be the most dangerous place in Afghanistan, according to the UN. But was staying in Pakistan as a perpetual refugee and doing nothing really any better? Especially if I had to stay alone? At least Kabul was my "home"—whatever that meant—and I could do my best to pick things up where I had left off.

First and foremost, I needed to find a job. From Quetta, I put out feelers with anyone I could think of; this notably included Radio Jawanan, the radio station for young people that had featured me on a program after Zohra returned from Davos. I wrote to them in English, and they replied enthusiastically, asking me to come in for an interview as soon as I got to Kabul. They made no promises, but at least I had a meeting scheduled. It was a start. I wasn't going back with no prospects at all. I also informed Dr. Sarmast of my impending return, but I would have to see once I got there if I could convince him to let me back into the ANIM.

After I'd begun turning all these options over in my mind, I started planning my trip. The simplest and cheapest solution was to go by road, in a shared taxi with my classmate Zulfiqar, his sister, Baran, and one of their friends. Their presence reassured my grandmother, who was concerned about the journey. We would have to go through Pashtun-inhabited regions crawling with Taliban fighters on both sides of the border. This was near the end of 2017, and at that time, the rebels often stopped buses and taxis and checked peoples' identity papers, pulling aside soldiers, policemen, civil servants, and occasionally Hazaras. Frequently, the soldiers would be killed, while the others were abducted and then either released or disappeared for good.

On the big day, Maha woke me up at midnight and made me sandwiches for the journey. I had already gotten my travel clothes ready the day before: a long green dress, pants, and a huge beige shawl wrapped around my body, completely covering me from head to toe. I thought I looked very elegant, in addition to being modestly covered up. Maha even gave me a surgical mask—usually used when we had a cold or the flu—to hide my face. (This would not seem uncommon now; since the Covid-19 pandemic began, everyone has them! But it was more unusual at the time.) She was terrified the Taliban would recognize me as the "bad girl" if they stopped us at the border. I took it but didn't end up wearing it. I adopted the attitude that what would be would be.

In addition to being a Hazara, I was, of course, traveling with my viola. This alone could increase my chances of attracting the Taliban's attention. How would I keep it away from their prying eyes? As I've said, the Taliban believe music to be ungodly and consider musicians, especially if they are girls, to be infidels. Thankfully, although I had arrived in Quetta with a single backpack, I was now leaving with a huge suitcase. My aunts had bought an entirely new wardrobe for my brothers and sister, and loads of beautiful outfits for me, too, although they were entirely unsuitable for Kabul. By a stroke of pure luck, my viola fit perfectly into the suitcase, and was hidden among the dresses, ruffles, and frills.

Despite Maha's protests—she was afraid that having an instrument would put me in grave danger—I didn't consider leaving it behind for a second. *If the Taliban kill me, it's just as well,* I thought to myself. I tried to be brave, but there was much uncertainty awaiting me.

I piled into the station wagon with my fellow passengers. My three travel companions and I were packed in the back, pressed up against each other. Two other people were up front, next to the driver. I sat by the window, listening to the music of Indian singer Arijit Singh to calm my nerves.

We arrived at the border a little before noon. There was already a huge crowd waiting to cross. I was overwhelmed at the sight of all these people standing among the porters and carts, moving in all directions through the dust and the stalls where steaming kebabs, bread, and hard-boiled eggs were sold. Here, a person had to get out of the car and walk to the checkpoint, leaving all their luggage with a porter. It was December and cold, but the sun was shining, which wasn't particularly helpful that day; we would have been much better off if it had been pouring with rain, because then we would have been practically invisible.

Despite the fear gripping my stomach, I followed the crowd, letting myself be carried along by them. There was nothing else for me to do now; the most important thing was to arrive safely on the other side.

We joined a line that was moving slowly forward, but I could only think about one thing: Where was our porter with the suitcases? Where was my viola? Zulfiqar tried to reassure me: "Don't worry about your stuff. It's probably already at the checkpoint." Disaster! I suddenly realized that they would search the bags and might find my viola. How would they react? What would happen? But it was too late to turn back. I knew I was taking a huge risk. I was also putting my friends in danger, because I hadn't, of course, told them about the viola. I'm sure they would have refused to travel with me if I had.

We went through passport control and then waited for our luggage. I was prepared to see someone jump out at any second and shout: "Which one of you is Zarifa?" Five minutes felt like five hours. Suddenly I saw the porter carrying my bag; it was open with my viola poking out from a bundle of clothes, after obviously having been thrown back in carelessly.

"Pay attention, would you! Look at what you're doing! That's important!" I shouted. I grabbed the viola and shoved it into my backpack as quickly as possible. The neck was sticking out of the top, and I covered it quickly with my long beige veil. But it was too late. The others were staring at me, dumbfounded.

"What in the world is that? Are you crazy?" cried Zulfiqar, glowering.

"Please, don't say anything. It's just my viola. It's hidden. It will be okay." I tried to act casual, as if it were the most natural thing in the world to travel around with a musical instrument, particularly in that Taliban-infested region. But everyone knew what was going on. Thankfully, nobody reacted. They were too preoccupied with their own concerns.

We went to the Afghan border post to cross the frontier on foot. In reality, it was just a demarcation line that had never been officially recognized by Kabul. The crossing was a short ten-minute walk, but it felt like an eternity to me, with my viola on my back and wide-eyed Pashtuns watching me as I passed.

We scrambled into a taxi and headed to the bus station, which was twenty minutes from the border. The taxi was some kind of pickup truck with no doors. The driver, clearly suspicious, kept staring at me in the rearview mirror.

"What's that on your knees?" he asked eventually, maybe thinking it was a weapon.

"Nothing, I promise. Nothing important."

The plan was to find a car at the bus station that would take us to the large city of Kandahar, and from there we would board a plane to Kabul. Traveling this way would take us longer than a more direct route, but this option, although not entirely without risk, did have the advantage of avoiding the more dangerous areas. Everyone at the bus station, from the drivers to the passengers themselves, seemed aggressive to me. Even the kids selling chewing gum, water, and boiled eggs were pushy and rude, shouting at customers: "Buy something!"

I clutched my viola tightly against me and kept it covered under my shawl. Zulfiqar ordered me and his sister to go inside the bus station and wait in the room reserved for women while he and his friend dealt with the rest of the luggage. Above all, I needed to be discreet. He quickly came back to get me and his sister, and together we got into a taxi bound for Kandahar.

Once we were on the road, I didn't dare let go of my instrument; I clung to it the whole way. I was terrified the Taliban would stop us and search the car. We told the driver to take us straight to the airport. The three other passengers were also Hazaras. One was very old, and the other two were tired and didn't pay any attention to us.

When we arrived at the airport three hours later, a relieved Zulfiqar could finally breathe easy again. He had been incredibly brave, calm, and supportive, hiding his fear of us all being arrested. And yet, we had taken an enormous risk. I also focused on breathing. Feeling conscious of the ordeal I had just put myself and—more importantly—my friends through, I didn't have much to say. At the baggage security check, the airport employee was suspicious: "What's that?" he demanded.

I answered him in a whisper. He sighed and rolled his eyes disapprovingly. But he let us through. On the plane, I put the instrument in the overhead luggage compartment, and an hour later, we landed in Kabul.

I took a taxi to the house. It was the first time I had been alone on the street with my viola; its weight on my back, a forbidden thrill, gave me renewed courage and energy. I was here. I had made the decision to come back with my viola. That choice, at least, was worth defending.

I got home in the late afternoon, and the place was, as ever, cold. Nothing had changed. Mom welcomed me, saying: "Thank God you're here!" Like every other time I had come back, she seemed genuinely happy to see me. That first evening, she even cooked for me, when usually it was the other way around. After that, everyone threw themselves on my suitcase to unpack its treasures.

It was a moment of pure joy for us all.

7

RADIO DJ IN KABUL

Had Mom really been sick? I'd seen no evidence of it since I'd arrived. I was simply happy to see her again, happy to go down with her to the courtyard to break up chunks of coal for the *bukhari* and bring it back up to our rooms on the fourth floor. It was exhausting work, the late December days were now bitterly cold, and the effort left us covered in black smears from head to toe. But we laughed as we worked. We were together. She needed me by her side. I finally understood that I was everything to her: her best friend, her punching bag, and her reason for living, despite the deep sorrow that ate away at her.

Feeling eager to sign a contract and start work, I met with the people in charge of Radio Jawanan the day after I returned to Kabul. I wore a jacket that was far too thin for the Kabul weather, and during the interview, I was numb with cold and felt slightly intimidated. Nonetheless, I found the courage to suggest that, since their target audience was the younger generation, they should launch a music program, during which they would take live calls from listeners who could ask questions or request their favorite songs. I was lucky; they happened to be looking for someone just like me. They were thrilled at the idea of a female DJ. Jackpot!

Aref, the production manager, a beautiful man with green eyes who was from Bamyan, warned me right away: "Traditionalist propaganda has no place here, either in the office or on air. And there is no discrimination between girls and boys, either."

If I couldn't return to the ANIM straightaway, I hoped that I would find a similar type of open-mindedness at the radio station and experience some kind of freedom. As it turned out, my worst fears about the ANIM were soon confirmed. I had a meeting with Dr. Sarmast, during which he informed me he couldn't let me come back.

As I stood in his office listening to him, I looked at the photos on the wall of the school's many orchestras and leaders, including a large photograph of Negin and photos of two boy conductors of the youth orchestra. But there were no photographs of me. I was glad that the orchestras were doing well, and I was happy for Negin and the other girls. But my absence in that place made me feel that maybe there was something wrong with me here, as well, just like I was made to feel all wrong at home. I wished there were at least a small photograph of me that showed I, too, had once belonged. I felt sad to no longer be included, and I felt that Dr. Sarmast had forgotten about me. So many people in my family had not valued me, and I couldn't help but feel that Dr. Sarmast no longer cared as much as he once had. And this hurt me very much.

He told me that my time away meant I was out of practice, both in terms of my viola playing and conducting. Everyone else had made progress since I'd left. He explained that new musicians had joined Zohra and that my friend Negin still conducted the group with much charm and grace. He made it clear that there was no longer a place for me in the orchestra. However, he offered to let me take viola lessons with an ANIM teacher for free.

"But bear in mind that with the pressures of work and the commute, it will be difficult," he warned. As for me, I made no secret of my strong desire to pursue further education as soon as possible and to attend an American university.

"You will have to choose," Dr. Sarmast insisted, not believing I could devote myself sufficiently to both music and my studies. My departure to Quetta remained a mystery to him, and he was still slightly suspicious. It would take him some time to realize I hadn't left on a mere whim.

At the radio station, Aref knew how important it was to resist, and he refused to let racism, sexism, or prejudice of any kind invade the premises of Radio Jawanan. That was good news for me because I, too, wanted to shake things up!

When I told him my story and shared my aspirations to study and be independent, he, in turn, confided in me. He told me how he had forced his parents to allow his young wife to continue her education after their wedding: "I didn't give them a choice. They didn't talk to me for two years! But today, you see, everything is fine!"

Aref would often joke around and was philosophical about the country's ills. "Afghanistan is the only country on earth where the past is better than the present!" he would say, laughing.

He wasn't wrong about Afghanistan's lack of progress. It's always been one step forward and two steps back in this country. He and I immediately agreed on what my role would be at the station. I would present a daily music program that would feature rock, pop, jazz, metal, rap, and other such genres. On Saturdays, I would talk about the lives of the musicians behind the music: everyone from the classical greats to contemporary superstars. The lineup I presented would be extensive and eclectic, designed to inspire lively debate among our young listeners. I would also help with the reporting for the news broadcasts.

The radio station's managers explained to me that their remit was to offer news, music, and sports. The mission was to provide entertainment for young people and help them forget the war, while also encouraging discussion, giving them a new perspective, and opening their eyes to the world. I could offer all of that with my confident words; my knowledge of English; and my quirky, rebellious side. And I also happened to know a thing or two about Western music!

I went on air for the first time on January 2, 2018, and my show was an immediate hit, particularly with the boys, who would call from all over the country to request their favorite songs.

"Hello, Afghanistaaaaan! Zarifa here! I'm delighted to be back for this latest installment of *Talkin' Music*!"

On Sunday shows, I also shared quotes from famous people, from Charlie Chaplin to Nelson Mandela. We had set up a Facebook page for the station that would announce our forthcoming programs and our quote of the day. I was particularly inspired by the hero of the anti-apartheid movement and by this line of Mandela's: "Do not judge me by my successes; judge me by how many times I fell down and got back up again." Another of his quotes that I shared, which continues to resonate with me to this day, was: "Education is the most powerful weapon which you can use to change the world."

Listeners would also suggest their own quotes, often taken from Persian poetry or from Rumi, the great poet and philosopher from Balkh, in the north, and one of the most widely read spiritual authors in the world. Young people from all around the country—from Kandahar, from Herat, from Khost—tuned in, some on a regular basis. One man even phoned in from prison.

The program was a real success. It was the breath of fresh air young people so badly needed. The girls grew bold and also started calling us up.

"It's Ramadan, and it's true that, theoretically, we should be listening to religious music," one said. "But there's so much sadness and suffering in this country." She wanted to hear something else. Many listeners did.

Of course, sometimes people would call in and criticize us: "What you're doing is wrong. The Quran forbids music. You are insulting God!"

But the threats were rarely serious enough to warrant interrupting the broadcast. All in all, everything went very smoothly. We would use a certain song, poem, or artist's biography as a springboard for discussion, and to encourage our youngsters. "Don't abandon your dreams," I would say. "Keep holding on to them even if it's hard!"

Some boys would openly flirt with me when they called—I even received two marriage proposals, live on air! Not to mention the propositions I received on Facebook. It made me laugh, it was harmless fun. But if one of them ever proved to be too insistent, which happened only rarely, we would cut off the call. Another time, a twenty-five-year-old musician I had invited to come on our weekly Monday program asked me to marry him after the show. My family had been wrong to worry about my prospects—now, I was drowning in proposals!

Generally, the listeners who requested songs, dedicating them to a friend—or to me!—chose Afghan artists like Aryana Sayeed and Ahmad Zahir, but callers also asked for a lot of Indian music. I, in turn, introduced them to Eminem and Adele.

I loved my job! When I was in the studio in front of the mike, I felt like I had been doing this my whole life. I had an audience again, even if they were invisible to me.

The radio station was located in an enormous traditional house that overlooked a rose garden. The house was at the top of a hill that could only be accessed via a well-worn road, and which had a clear view of the city. The house's owners had originally used it as a movie studio to film episodes of a famous police series. That had been during Kabul's golden age: in the wake of the Americans' arrival, cash had flowed in, and people had been craving light entertainment after being repressed by the Taliban's regime for so long. The city opened up; the country was reborn. But there wasn't much filming being done anymore. The leisure economy, like everything else, was now failing.

I was learning something new every day: how to manage the archives, how to prepare my shows, how to write news reports . . . and so it went on. The bosses trusted me, and, bit by bit, we became close friends. However, the atmosphere within the team, which was young and diverse, wasn't as laid-back and open as I had expected.

At first glance, my female colleagues, who were all in their twenties, had seemed friendly. But I found it difficult to join in on their conversations. They still thought of me as somewhat of a misfit, and my habit of speaking and acting so freely, uncensored, bothered them. I was sad to see that they remained so stuck in their beliefs. I must have seemed like a real rebel in comparison. They would constantly whisper and gossip behind my back. My appearance, my clothes, my attitude . . . perhaps what they saw as my arrogance: everything about me seemed to baffle them, and they made snide remarks at the least excuse.

"You're not wearing your headscarf?" one of them inquired almost as soon as I started working there.

These women always had something to say to me about the Quran or Islam, and about how to pray, dress, and act—as if they knew the religious texts, and even God, more intimately and far better than I did. The boys weren't any different. One of them, in particular, was so ridiculous that I enjoyed provoking him for fun. He hosted the news and sports program. He was twenty-seven years old and had been to university, but despite his youth and modern upbringing, he was terribly conservative. One day, I was listening to music with my headphones on, as usual, so I wouldn't hear my colleagues gossiping, when Esmatullah came up to me and declared: "You spend too much time listening to music. It's haram—forbidden."

I felt like reminding him that he, too, worked for a radio station that broadcast both news and music! Apparently, he preferred to forget that little detail. He liked the job and needed the income, but he also wanted to spare his conscience.

"Sorry, but where did you get that idea?" I asked him. This was my pet subject: a topic I discussed often with my teachers and my friends.

"It's in the Quran, obviously! Also, I can see your hair. Cover it up. It is tempting me to sin, and so are you!"

I was tempting him to sin. What if he just ignored me? I went right ahead and suggested the idea to him: "So don't look at me, then! And show me where that's written in the Quran."

He persisted, the poor thing. "If the mullahs say it, it must be true. They know."

I lost my temper. "How can those corrupt old men know what's haram and what isn't?"

We would clearly never agree. Things got even worse when he found out I was a musician. One day in the spring, I had a lesson scheduled at the ANIM after work, so I arrived at the office with my viola on my back. This also appeared to annoy him.

"Get it out of my sight!" Esmatullah spat with disgust. "I can't sit next to that. I would be an accomplice in your crime!" His reaction was so stupid I had to stifle my laughter.

As summer approached and the temperature got hotter and hotter, I grumbled about a society that forced us girls to cover ourselves from head to toe, including our arms, whenever we went out in public. Meanwhile, boys could go to work wearing short-sleeved shirts.

One day, I arrived at the studio in the middle of a heat wave with the sleeves of my dress rolled up to my elbows. Yes, that's right, *up to my elbows*. My forearms were exposed. How shocking! Fawzia, a colleague who sometimes read the news, came up to me and discreetly pulled my sleeves down. When I protested, she kindly whispered to me: "Zarifa, you know we're in Afghanistan and that we're girls. That's just the way things are. Be careful: everyone is talking about you behind your back and criticizing you."

Despite the wishes of the radio station's founders, it remained difficult to change people's attitudes, even in 2018. I had hoped that among young people who were educated, I would encounter open-mindedness instead of this resignation. It was obvious to me that it was going to be increasingly difficult to find my place in this city, in this country.

In order to keep the peace and avoid trouble, women had generally stopped questioning the moral code imposed on them and had accepted their status in a system that gave them less freedom than men. They didn't even consider questioning things, at least not openly. "That's just the way it is" was a common refrain. And as for rebellion? Forget it. These women sounded like my mother. Their fatalism was exhausting.

I realized that in the face of this I was becoming tougher and increasingly stubborn. I had made enough concessions at home and with my family; here at the radio station, I considered it simply out of the question. This radio station, this job, was my source of freedom. What's more, our very aim in broadcasting to youngsters was to both entertain and educate. I ended up isolating myself from the rest of the team and would no longer talk to them. I spent most of my time with my headphones on and even turned my desk around so I could sit facing the window with my back to the room.

Only a few boys on the team continued to chat and joke with me. They were in their twenties and were funny and laid-back, dressing in jeans and shirts. We would have lunch together sitting on the benches in the garden or inside near the stove. This only confirmed what the others thought they knew: I was a lost cause.

Fortunately, I was lucky to have the support of my superiors, who were in charge of both the station and its programming. They stayed the course and were faithful to their commitments. My bosses even suggested I move up to their floor. They knew they weren't going to change all of Afghan society with a couple of radio shows, but they thought that if I worked alongside them I could at least avoid hearing the team's sarcastic remarks.

Sadly, after my return to Kabul, I saw very little of my friends from the ANIM. They were all busy with their own lives and activities: Shiraz was in college, and Samir was working at the RTA, the public television channel. Of the four of us, Samim was the only one still attending the music school, along with Negin, of course, who was continuing with her conducting and piano studies. It didn't help that the violence surging through the city had forced all of us to limit our outings to the bare minimum. But I managed to stay in contact with all of them, especially Samir, who I would meet up with from time to time.

It was difficult for me to get away, though. At home, the honeymoon period with my mother hadn't lasted very long. Whenever she wasn't feeling well, or if something went wrong or upset her, it didn't matter what the cause was, she would take it out on me. Just like before. I was still her "problem" and she treated me as such: "You are a burden. The worst mistake I ever made. You should never have been born."

These moments were brutal, but they had happened so many times before that I gradually taught myself to remain unmoved by her outbursts. I had never dared say it to her face, but I would often think to myself: *All of that's your problem! I never asked for any of this. You're the one who gave birth to me, and now I'm here!*

These episodes tore me apart. Her words pierced me like knives. No one had ever taught her that a mother's tongue could do harm and, worse still, even destroy. So, it was up to me to lick my wounds and rise above it all, because she would never change, if only because of her pride.

My mother still struggled to cope on her meager budget, and she remained under the constant watchful gaze of her in-laws. She was also annoyed that I left home early every morning to go to the radio station. A good girl would never do that! A good girl would never leave the house to go work with men.

She would have liked to forbid me, but she couldn't afford to. She needed my salary. I earned two hundred forty dollars a month, from which I would take five hundred afghanis (less than eight dollars) to pay for my transport. Whenever possible, I would also put aside ten dollars for my savings account. I was now the one who paid for the children's school and bus fees, and I helped feed the household.

I realized this situation bothered her. She seemed to resent the fact that she was dependent on me. Our relationship quickly became as unstable and unpredictable as it had been before. And whenever I tried to argue that I needed an outing, a breath of fresh air, she thought I was being arrogant. "Just because you're bringing money in, you think you can do whatever you want? You think you can talk to me like that?"

Basir, her husband, still hadn't sent any money, and his visa applications didn't seem to be going anywhere. One night, after he called her from Indonesia, she lost her temper: "He's out there sleeping all day, while you are doing everything!"

Basir sent little news, but, even worse, by not providing for us, he was humiliating his family. Anis Gul and her children had become second-class citizens within the family. I felt like the family wanted me to pay for the person they thought I was: an orphan, a rebel, a troublemaker, someone who was so free-spirited she couldn't possibly be honest. Naturally, most of the time, they didn't say any of this to my face. Everything went through my mother, who was finding their complaints increasingly difficult to put up with.

They should have been happy. I was no longer a part of the Zohra Orchestra. A first step in the right direction, one might have expected them to think. But it was no use trying to please them.

At home, I sensed the Uncles were ready to ambush me. On top of working at the station, I had to look after the house: polishing; sweeping; doing the laundry; and cleaning the floor, walls, and carpets. This was the same situation faced by most girls who wanted to study. I would often leave at six in the morning; in the evening, by the time I had taken several minibuses across the city, I would get home no earlier than seven o'clock, long after dark, and have to do my chores then. I bent over backward trying to fit the mold, trying to stay invisible, to buy myself a little freedom. But I was still the black sheep of the family in their eyes.

What was there to be done? The best way to get rid of me was obvious to them, once again: marry me off to a husband who would know how to tame me. The first "fiancé" they had found for me almost a year ago, shortly after my return from Davos—the mechanic from Ghazni—had been a trial run. He'd been a distant relative who would have been acceptable to all—except me! That choice would have reassured Mom by shutting everyone else up, and it would have rid the family of my presence.

We were soon introduced to the second potential husband. This time, it wasn't a relative but a boy from the neighborhood, and his mother knew mine. Whenever women in our city judged it was the right time to find a bride for their sons, they started looking around for the best possible candidate. This process involved contacting their immediate circle of family and friends, people with good reputations, to see if anyone had a daughter of a suitable age. In the past, they would even use the hammam—a public bath—as an opportunity to look out for young, beautiful women and evaluate their . . . qualities.

First, the new potential husband's mother had shown up, alone, to ask for my hand in marriage. Then, both parents and their son all came back together, as was the custom. Generally, girls are only introduced to their fiancé once negotiations are already well underway, but Mom was already singing his praises. She swore he was the perfect boy for me. I didn't even know what he did for a living, but she was very sure of her choice, and flattered, too, that he and his family were interested in me. She kept telling me all the good things about this family. She could already see herself as a mother-in-law, presiding over our wedding, and as a soon-to-be grandmother with her arms full of babies. The image was a wonderful restorative for her.

Since the first attempt to marry me off, which had been quickly abandoned, I had remained fairly calm, despite my anger. But this time,

I started getting really scared once I saw how determined they all were. I had gone to Quetta for more than half a year, but that hadn't been long enough for them to cool off. Quite the opposite. The Uncles and my mother were still obsessed with wanting me to marry.

I felt very alone in this ordeal and was in desperate need of Mom's support. I longed for her to be on my side for once. I think that's what hurt me the most: seeing her so enthusiastic over this prospect. I knew I had to do everything I could to convince her to leave me alone, even if it was difficult for her to accept my desire to remain single. I was already almost twenty years old. All the girls in the family had been married or at least engaged by my age. I was going to be left behind. How awful! Mom was increasingly worried, and tongues had started wagging: "Ah look, Anis Gul's daughter still isn't married. What's wrong with her?"

I tried to negotiate and reason with my mother. Then I even mustered up the courage to confront her directly: "Mom, do you really want to condemn me to the same fate as you? Were you happy to be married off too young to someone you didn't love?"

"That's how things are, Zarifa. You'll be twenty soon; at your age, I'd already had you. Wait any longer and you'll be too old. No one will want you anymore."

The shame, the dishonor! The idea of me going to university still didn't make any sense to her. I certainly didn't confess to her my secret dream of going to law school and studying for a PhD—at Harvard if possible! She didn't understand what studying actually meant. All those years that would be wasted. What was the point if I was still single? What good would any of it do me when it came to raising a family and obeying my husband? I'd had my period of freedom with my music, and now it was time to move on. She was so looking forward to being a grandmother. I could understand where she was coming from. But why me? Would I always be the one who had to sacrifice her own hopes and dreams for the future?

I was by no means the only one facing this situation. After the orchestra returned from Davos, three girls from Zohra left the ANIM and Kabul. Two of them had chosen to get married; one of them has a little girl now. The third was forced to return to her parents' house in Nangarhar: a conservative eastern province that was hotly fought over by the Taliban and by ISIS, who had their headquarters there. My friend disappeared soon after. She simply vanished. We never heard from her again. It's likely she was married off, too. In any case, studying and music were over for all three of them. The idea that I would suffer the same fate petrified me. But how could I resist such pressure?

In the end, I managed to get rid of that marriage candidate, as well. When we finally met, I didn't even greet his parents. My mother nearly exploded afterward.

According to them, my behavior showed an inexcusable lack of respect. And yet, against all odds, my rejection of him seemed to finally make Mom come around. Or maybe I should just say she finally gave up. Her nagging had its limits, whereas my obstinacy didn't.

By now, my cousins now suspected that I had a "boyfriend," the ultimate stain on a girl's reputation. Mom also dreaded the possibility of this happening, but she trusted me that, so far, it hadn't. My cousins believed this silly rumor because of the "bad girl" video, my studies at the music school, and my job at the radio station, where I didn't hide that I had both girls and boys as friends. Since I didn't have a computer, I could only contact my friends via Facebook when I was at the radio station. The social media site was my only link to the outside world, my escape. I continued to receive encouraging messages from strangers who had seen my interview or read press articles about me. "Hang in there. This country needs more girls like you," some would say.

Relations remained more strained than usual between me and my family, and the recurring arguments between my mother and elder brother Ahmad didn't help. One evening, I was so exasperated I ran away from home and sought refuge with some foreign girlfriends of mine, who lived on the other side of the city. They panicked when they saw me arrive in the middle of the night, in mid-February, but were even more worried about what would happen to me when I returned home the next day. But once I did, it was as if the family had hardly noticed I was gone. Did anyone in this world actually care about me? I sensed they were far more anxious about preserving their reputations than about my well-being.

One evening, I summoned the courage to talk to Uncle Haider, who was still the eldest member and head of the family: "Uncle, I am my mother's eldest daughter. I want to be like a son to her. That's why I need to continue my education. My dream is to go to Yale or Harvard." I explained to him what these great American universities represented, the prestige and the respect. "I want to study international relations and law so I can work and be independent later on. I want to fight for girls, for women. Please, let me go."

For the first time in my life, I had shown him what I was, who I was. He listened to me, impassive. Yet, he seemed surprised by my boldness and sincerity. I knew this because he neither looked away nor interrupted me.

"Who will pay? You know I won't give you a penny!"

"Obviously not. I'll figure it out on my own. I'll do everything I can to get a scholarship. You'll all be proud of me, you'll see. I'll take care of Mom and pay for my brothers' and sister's tuition. You won't have to worry about us anymore."

Uncle Haider raised his eyebrows at this and said: "Well, if you want to study for your entrance exams . . . you can stay until the summer. Just don't bring shame to the family. And remember, you are at the age when you will have to get married soon."

I accepted, of course. I kissed his hands as a sign of respect and submission: "Thank you, Uncle. You can count on me."

In the end, my only regret was that I hadn't had this conversation with him sooner.

8

IF I WERE A BOY

Sometimes, I have regretted not having been born a boy. Afghan society, through its traditions and the efforts of those who interpret religion without truly studying it or understanding the scriptures, has turned girls into "problems": a vast reservoir of temptation ready to sully men's honor and draw them into sin at any given moment. I feel certain that if I had been born a boy, I would have been respected and more easily accepted. I had so many things I wanted to do to make things better: for girls, for my mother, for Afghanistan. During those middle teen years, being a girl felt like a mountain I had to climb. I would have done anything to have the power to help others. I couldn't imagine any way to do that outside of being a boy, and if I could have wished myself one then, I would have done so.

If I'd been a male child, I would have been able to play music without having to hide. The Uncles wouldn't have forced us to come and live with them when my stepfather went to Indonesia. Plus, nobody pays attention to what a boy wears. No one cares whether he has on his *kamiz* tunic, pants, or turban, or whether his clothes are neat and clean. People don't concern themselves with whether a boy has short or long hair, if he leaves early and comes home late, or if he swims or plays soccer. If I were a boy, my environment, my society, would have allowed me to make decisions and act as I saw fit. My mother never would have kicked me out of the house, and my stepfather certainly wouldn't have disowned me. I also would have found a job more easily, there's no doubt about that.

And what about my mother? Would she have been better off if her firstborn child had been a son? Her in-laws would have preferred it, that's for sure. When my brother Ali, her first son, was born, the family took their guns out of the safe to celebrate the birth, shooting at the sky with joy.

"Everyone took care of me," she recalled of that day. "I stayed in bed for ten days and didn't have to lift a finger."

Poor Mom, things were very different when my sister Najla was born! No one came to visit her at the maternity ward. She stayed there for barely two days before Basir whisked her home, where she promptly got back to work.

Even now, baby girls are still frequently abandoned, even in Kabul. During those tumultuous years, did my mother ever wonder if she would have been better off without me? Sons are a boost to the ego and provide the mother with status, but daughters stay at home and help with the housework.

What's more, parents usually rely on their sons to support them financially. But I, a daughter, had learned to fulfill that role a long time ago. I was essentially the head of my mother's family, managing the house as well as bringing in a little money. I had learned to support my mother, to deal with her tantrums and bouts of depression, while also taking care of my younger siblings. Even if it was true that she still took my brothers down to eat kebabs at the restaurant, leaving Najla and me behind, I was now essentially the "man" at her side.

There were times during the months following my return to Kabul, after my stay in Quetta, when I had felt like running away from her.

I even tried to convince myself I didn't love her. But that wasn't true. And for a girl, I was actually doing quite well for myself. Little by little, I was acquiring my independence. Nothing was easy, but I was on top of things; I was working and mentally preparing myself for college. I hadn't given up on any of my dreams.

But when people pursue dreams and stay true to themselves, it can be uncomfortable and seem to cause trouble for the people around them. And so the hard feelings in my family continued. The fact that I'd refused my second prospective husband only made things more tense.

One night, Ali confronted me: "Everyone is angry because of you, Zarifa; you cause too much trouble." At that moment, I felt mad at him for being so selfish. Especially since I knew that, deep down, he supported me. He had even gotten upset one Friday when he saw me scrubbing a large carpet on the roof all by myself. "That's enough! She does enough already!" he had exclaimed.

But he was young, only fourteen years old. And when it comes to families, it's always the odd one out who ends up being rejected: the one who causes a scene, the one who shouts, the one who ruins the mood and transforms family meals into verbal boxing matches. Everyone wants an easy life, and so they keep the peace by hiding behind a facade of family unity. I had already sensed this dynamic and discussed it with my aunt Maha during my exile in Quetta. Ali strenuously avoided getting involved in any matters that were marriage related—all of that was for the women. He even joked about the situation afterward and pretended to miss the suitors and their gifts, saying, "It's a shame you've stopped receiving marriage proposals, Zarifa. I liked it when they brought fruit baskets!"

Najla, however, didn't ever talk about it. The thought of being next in line seemed to terrify her. She had observed everything in silence, without commenting or talking to me about it. But one day, I came home early to find her stuffing herself with food. She had just finished a plate of rice and was now devouring a large slab of bread, methodically biting off huge mouthfuls and chewing them one by one.

"What's gotten into you? You're going to be the size of a house! Do you remember what I looked like at your age?"

"Look, in this country, men like thin girls. So, I thought that if I get fat, no one will want me and I won't have to get married," was her reply.

"Stop it, you're hurting yourself! You just need to tan a little, that'll do the trick. Afghans don't like dark skin. Put on some cream and go lie in the sun, you'll see!" I told her, laughing.

All jokes aside, this reasoning betrayed her fears and broke my heart. Without ever having said anything, my strong and beautiful Najla had devised her own strategies for escaping a potential forced marriage.

I was looking for my sister the next day when Mom told me she had spent the whole day on the roof and had turned crimson.

"I was only kidding, Najla! You're all sunburned, look at you!" I exclaimed.

"I did what you said. No one will want me once I'm really dark," she answered.

But despite her words, she regretted her choice. Nothing Mom did could soothe her livid red face. Kabul's high altitude meant that the sun was especially brutal there. Girls were clearly willing to try anything to escape marriage. Najla's tactics were something we were able to joke about. But in the most desperate of cases, some girls ran away or even set themselves on fire.

Ever since Najla had turned thirteen, my mother, under pressure from the family, had forbidden her from running around like she usually did when I would take her for a walk around the parks. "She's too old for that sort of thing," declared the Uncles.

Yet it wasn't as if she was running around with her arms bare or wearing mini-shorts. The real reason for forcing the vast majority of girls to avoid sport of any kind lay elsewhere. The theory went that by running, jumping, or even cycling, girls risked tearing their hymen and thus "losing" their sacrosanct virginity. This result would mean certain dishonor for her family when the day came to display the sheets from the wedding night. The notion that sports could deflower a girl was deeply ingrained in our society, especially among the working classes. The Afghan women who, despite everything, participated in the few running or cycling competitions they were allowed to enter—such as the Bamyan marathon, which took place each year in November, under the watchful eyes of the province's ancient Buddhas—would train in secret before sunrise.

One day, I'd gotten a taste of this treatment myself, when I mounted a bicycle in the courtyard at the ANIM. I was reprimanded by the old janitor: "Zarifa, get down from there right away!" He was truly distraught. I complained to Dr. Sarmast, who subsequently warned Mahmoud to leave us alone and not interfere with our personal lives.

Even more recently, at the radio station, several girls had screamed in horror when they saw me jumping off a bench: "Zarifaaaaa! You're crazy!" It was always the same obsession. They had grown up with it and hadn't ever thought of questioning it themselves. As long as these attitudes persisted, the consequences of resisting them were too dire to think about. Woe to the girl whose wedding sheets remained spotless. She risked the immediate repudiation of her marriage. And who knew how her father and brothers would react to that?

Najla was so attached to her Olympic dream, she found various ways of getting around this rule about running. I did my part by pretending to take her to the bazaar when, really, we were going to the park. At home, she would run circuits around the roof and constantly trot all over the house, between the kitchen and the dining room, or she'd simply run in one spot. When I made fun of her for this, she reminded me of a girl she knew who used to practice her scales on a paper keyboard and who'd played a stick in place of a viola. Touché. We all have our own dreams.

I continued to pursue mine by working at the radio station: an experience that taught me many things. One day, in preparation for a feature we were doing for the radio program, I went to visit the ArtLords: a name that identified the participants as lords of art rather than of war. This was a group of artists and community activists who introduced young people to painting by covering Kabul's blast-proof T-walls with abstract murals.

The committed Afghan artists who'd created ArtLords in 2014 had been quickly joined by many young volunteers. The organization wanted to hold the authorities accountable; develop a culture of social awareness and responsibility; and fight against corruption, impunity, and injustice. They used their highly visible artwork on Kabul's T-walls to denounce domestic violence, as well as the favoritism and corruption of the system; to promote the importance of public health and hygiene (such as washing one's hands and consulting a doctor); and to explain the benefits of education, respect, vaccination of infants, and peace.

It also just so happened that I had been depicted on one of the murals: it had shown us, the girls of the Zohra Orchestra, gathered around Dr. Sarmast.

When I arrived to interview the members of the group, they were painting a "cloud of wishes," and Omaid Sharifi, one of the founders, invited me to write down the first one. I took the paintbrush and wrote: *I wish people would see me as a human being before seeing me as a girl.*

"Fantastic! I'm very proud of you—what a great wish," he exclaimed enthusiastically.

I asked him why they had painted Zohra's portraits on the governor's wall downtown, to which he responded: "But you have no idea! You, as musicians, have done more for this country than any politician!"

"Thank you, Omaid jan," I said. (The diminutive "jan" is a word that is added to a name to express affection and respect.) "But I almost lost my family over it. I was even forced to leave my country."

Omaid and the artist Kabir Mokamel—I call him "Lala Kabir"—were founding members of the ArtLords, and they both became my great friends. Lala Kabir also became my mentor. They, along with Dr. Sarmast and the teachers at the ANIM, as well as Chris Stone, the Australian musician who visited the ANIM in 2014 and who became a faithful supporter and friend of mine, were among the men who were there for me. Together, these were my friends, advisers, spiritual guides, sources of inspiration, and surrogate fathers—I knew I could talk to them about anything. Whenever I was struggling, they told me: "It's okay. You're exactly where you're supposed to be. Feel your emotions." Once, Lala Kabir told me: "Zarifa, when you are going through something, feel all your feelings, with all your soul. Feel them, be friends with them, and then try to let them go. Actually, you won't even have to try. They will go after you've let them in. You won't have to fight them anymore."

They were always there for me.

For a long time, I had distrusted men in general. Those that had been around me had been too toxic, or simply indifferent. I didn't have a role model or hero to look up to. I couldn't begin to imagine falling in love. If I ever spoke about the possibility of marriage, it was only to be deliberately provocative. I claimed I would marry a Pashtun, or a Tajik, to show that I was willing to ignore these ethnic divides. But most of the time, I refused to think about love.

At that moment in time, however, and more than ever, I needed to find some new role models. And so, whenever I was at the radio station and had access to the internet, I would take the opportunity to listen to Michelle Obama or Nelson Mandela speak. I would also watch American TV talk shows, such as Ellen DeGeneres's *The Ellen Show* or Oprah Winfrey. It was on *Ellen* that I first came across an interview with Malala Yousafzai: the young Pakistani girl who had been seriously injured by the Taliban in 2012 as she protested in support of girls' right to education. Awarded the Nobel Peace Prize at the age of seventeen—by far the youngest of any laureate—Malala explained that before the attack, her biggest fear had been that the Taliban would come and kill her.

"When they shot me, they took that fear away. Ever since the worst has happened, I am not afraid of anything anymore!"

As she pronounced those words, her whole face lit up. That made me think. I had also been living in fear, for the last three years at least. At home and in the street. I'd felt the fear of being discovered when I was playing with the Zohra Orchestra, the fear of upsetting my mother, the fear of being prevented from going to school. And after everyone found out I was the "bad girl," the musician who'd supposedly showed off in Davos, I'd become afraid of being assaulted in the street, of being forced to marry, of not being able to go to university, of disappearing entirely.

How can we change things so that girls, all girls, no longer need to be afraid? How can we protect girls from a fate similar to the one that threatened Sonita Alizadeh, a rapper from Herat who was nearly sold into marriage at the age of sixteen? This cause became her battle, and rap—which she discovered thanks to artists like Eminem—her weapon. After fleeing to Iran, she was granted asylum in the United States, where she continues to condemn the sale of young girls into these barbaric marriages.

Worse still, who could forget Farkhunda Malikzada's tragic fate? The horrific circumstances surrounding her death in March 2015 shocked Afghanistan and the world. Women even took to the streets of Kabul. The way that she was killed made a huge impression on me, one that remains with me to this day. I can't ever forget what happened to her, and I should not. As horrible as it is to do so, remembering what happened to her is important, both to honor her and to keep in mind why we all have to work so hard to make things different for the girls of Afghanistan.

What was the "crime" Farkhunda Malikzada supposedly committed? This young twenty-seven-year-old Muslim woman, a scholar with a degree in Islamic sciences, had criticized the sale of talismans in front of a famous shrine. The seller and guardian of the holy site, seeking revenge, accused her of burning a Quran. The false accusation provoked the fury of the crowd, made up of fifty to sixty men—some of them my own age.

Farkhunda was lynched, dragged through the streets, crushed, and beaten to death. She was punched and kicked. One young man my age even stomped on her while she was on the ground.

When they were done beating her, the men threw her brutalized body into a dry riverbed and burned her to death while she was still alive. All this occurred under the impassive gazes of numerous onlookers, some of whom even filmed the scene, and of the police, who made no real effort to put a stop to the carnage.

Over the years, I have wondered: Did she feel all that brutality? Did she ask God to take her pain away? Or did her body fall unconscious, sparing her at least some of the pain? And there are other questions: What mentality must the men in that Afghan crowd have had for them to have abused a young woman so violently? The Afghanistan I love is beautiful. But this horrific act toward Farkhunda is Afghanistan, too. I don't know how to reconcile the two.

A few months after Farkhunda's death, a nineteen-year-old girl identified only as Rokhsahana, who had been forced to marry an older man, was stoned to death by the clerics of her province and by the Taliban for having run away with her lover. The singer Aryana Sayeed, our very own Afghan pop star, even wrote a song about these tragedies. Each time she performed it, she would be on the verge of tears, raising her fists in the air and standing in front of the images of tortured girls projected in the background. The mullahs issued a fatwa against Aryana, who had grown up in Europe, and as a result, she returned to London to live and was placed under high protection whenever she visited Kabul. But she pushed through her fears and kept coming back.

I thought about these things all the time. Once again, I concluded that the only possible way out for us, for me and all the other girls, was education. I even came to believe that it was for the sake of this cause that I had been born where I was born, and that I was meant to take on this challenge. It was up to me to be smart enough to make sure success in education was achieved. After all, Afghanistan already had a women's orchestra, a women's cycling team, and a women's rock-climbing team, as well as high-school-aged girls from Herat who were finalists in the world robotics championships. Other women were going into business. Anything was possible. Especially since most of these girls were Hazaras, like me.

Ever since my short stay at Yale, I had become more determined than ever to attend one of the great American universities. I remained tormented by this idea, especially since I no longer had the freedom that the ANIM and its concerts offered me. But I had a plan. I went to the American University of Afghanistan (AUAF) in Kabul to inquire about their admissions schedule, and I discovered that the date of the entrance examination was approaching. I had to obtain a scholarship—the tuition fees were far too expensive for me to afford. Nothing but these goals mattered. This was my passport to the future. From AUAF, I could envisage continuing my higher education abroad.

I prepared for the exam whenever I could squeeze in some study time between the radio station, my viola lessons at the ANIM, and my chores at home. I had a few girlfriends who worked for the United Nations or other humanitarian organizations who taught me how to write essays in English. They also suggested that I apply to the American University of Central Asia (AUCA) in Bishkek, Kyrgyzstan, rather than staying in Kabul. The AUCA was another American campus, created after the fall of the USSR in the 1990s, and reserved for students from the region.

I liked the prospect of leaving Afghanistan and getting away from the family, and so I met up with these girlfriends as frequently as I could, often on Friday afternoons, in a café located in an old house in the center of Kabul. They would motivate me and help me with my revisions. The espresso coffees, the fresh juices, the lemon and chocolate cakes all gave the place an exotic aroma, and being there almost felt like being on vacation. The regulars would call out to each other from one table to the next or greet each other with a kiss. The well-kept café provided a comforting respite from the hellish chaos of the city. The boys and girls who hung out there fascinated me. Many had studied abroad, and some already worked in various ministries or large international agencies. I wanted to be like them.

As the AUAF entrance exams got closer, a new obstacle arose: my identity papers had disappeared. Najla came to my aid, and together we turned the house upside down: drawer after drawer, closet after closet. Nothing.

When my mother came home from the market that day, I asked her for help. But just at that moment, Najla called down to me from the roof. She had just discovered the charred remains of my passport. My identity card, or *tazkira*, meanwhile, was nowhere to be found. It had probably been burned as well. Who could have done such a thing? The only people in the house who were dead set against me studying were my mother, my uncle, and my cousins. I began to interrogate my mother. I was distraught and completely panicked. The exams were in a few days. Without any official documentation, I would never be able to register.

"Who did this, Mom, who?!" I could barely stop myself from shouting.

"Your Uncles' wives or your cousins," she said eventually. "Please don't say anything. Don't cause a scene."

Around the same time, my very first diary was taken from its hiding place in a drawer and thrown on the floor, and I found the few family photos I owned, including the only one I had of my father, scattered on the carpet. I felt more certain than ever: I had to wrench myself away from here. These people would never go easy on me. They would never let me live in peace or make my own decisions.

Fortunately, there was still hope for university. With the help of a girlfriend, I obtained a waiver that allowed me to sit the exams even without proving my identity.

Shortly after this incident, I found one of the rare pictures that had been taken of me as a child, with my short bob, torn into three jagged pieces. I'm four years old in the picture. I've got round cheeks and I'm wearing a little blue dress. I'm looking up, staring seriously at the photographer—my grandfather perhaps? I'm cute. There are other children in the photo, too: cousins on my mother's side. She remembers that the photo was taken in Pakistan during a family trip.

I had kept the picture in my diary, pressed between some dried flowers. Now there it was, all torn up. As if to conceal me, to erase my existence. Based on the location of the rips, a person could almost put two of the pieces back together without me, omitting me completely. Someone had left the ruined photo in my diary. Who would go through my drawers just to rip up a photo? The act was too childish for an adult. I thought this more likely to be the work of a cousin.

This picture had been one of three photos I possessed, which, together, constituted the sole artifacts I had of my childhood. In the second photo, I'm one year old, asleep on my mother's lap while she stares into the distance. It was my favorite; she looked absolutely beautiful in it. In the third one—taken before 2012—my two half-brothers Bilal and Fahim, who at the time I thought were my cousins, are standing on either side of me.

At the time, they already knew I was their sister. What had they been thinking in that moment? Why hadn't they said anything? What were they afraid of? Had they been told to stay silent? After I found the ripped-up photograph, I impassively placed the three shredded pieces in my diary and put it back in the drawer. What was the use of getting angry or, worse, crying? I wouldn't give whoever did it the satisfaction.

Soon after, there was another incident: I found two of my favorite dresses at the bottom of a trash can. Who could have done something so nasty? The clothes weren't worth very much, but I wore them all the time. They were short tunic dresses, one pink, the other dark blue, that I would wear over a shirt or T-shirt with leggings. It was such a hostile and petty thing to do. I naturally suspected my cousins—that vicious lot. They got everything they wanted without ever having to work, but at the end of the day, I didn't envy them. I didn't care what they did, as long as they left me alone.

I wiped my eyes. What did it matter? To comfort myself, I imagined my future. I would dress however I pleased and would even have my own "personal designer," like *Michelle*. I felt better already.

As always, what hurt me the most was not having someone to protect me. If only my father—my "real" father—were here, by my side, I thought, they wouldn't have dared. Even if Basir had stayed with us, this void would have probably felt a little less harsh. When he was still around, I hadn't felt the need for a man who was a ghost in my life. But everything had changed the moment Basir made a distinction between "his" children and me, his wife's daughter.

I was about to turn twenty, though. It was time to stop looking for a father in every man I met. I had to move on, let go of this obsession that was getting me nowhere. However, after I came home from the radio station one evening, one of my older uncles called me into his living room and sat me down. He had never gotten along with Haider and had always treated me well. Yet, I was still tense, and wondered what was going to happen to me.

"Zarifa, I had a dream last night. Your father appeared to me, he was upset, and he ordered me to talk to you. He told me, 'My daughter has to know who I am,' and I felt bad. I thought that if I died, right then and there, I would probably go to hell. So, tell me, what would you like to know?" he said.

The family was so superstitious. They saw omens everywhere. A throbbing right eye was a good sign, but if it was the left one, it was bad. Foot pain, an eyelash on your cheekbone—all of it meant something. My mother, in particular, kept an eye out for these signs, as she believed they could cause real harm. So, dreaming of a dead man was a warning if ever there was one! My uncle preferred not to take any risks.

That evening, he tried to bring his younger brother to life in my presence for the very first time. He described my father as a tall, handsome man of great kindness, a *charshana*. He was a good-looking man with a soft gaze and a fair complexion.

"He could have been mistaken for a Pashtun," my uncle assured me. "He was brave, honest, and hardworking—in fact, he supported the whole family, looking after everyone's needs. He was our parents' favorite son."

My father, the favorite son?! Nothing could have made me happier. There I was, finally anchored by a happy lineage. For the first time, I was learning about my origins, and it was in laudatory terms. This uncle had just taken an enormous weight off of my shoulders. I was almost twenty years old, and I had finally found out that my father had been good, loved, and respected while he was alive. He would have spoiled me and protected me, and I would have made him proud.

My mother, on the other hand, continued to avoid my questions. She had not kept any photos of him. The only one I could find was the result of some clever scissor work. One day, as I was looking at a photo of my half-brothers Ahmad, Bilal, and Fahim, I saw a frame hanging on the wall in the background behind them. The photograph in that frame was of our father! I delicately cut that smaller photograph out, and that was how I acquired my first portrait of him. It was the size of a postage stamp.

I stared at it and memorized every detail. His face had been carefully retouched, giving him a sheer complexion and a well-defined pink mouth. The picture had been taken by a professional in a studio. My father was staring at the photographer with quiet assurance. He had a neatly trimmed mustache and wore a golden silk turban, one side of which was draped, impeccably folded, on his left shoulder. Throughout the years, I kept this small picture like a talisman.

Then one day at the end of Ramadan, while I was visiting my older brother Ahmad to celebrate Eid al-Fitr, I finally came across the original. I arrived and greeted everyone with *"Eid Mubarak,"* and my thirteen-year-old niece brought me tea, nuts, and cakes. She had always been nice to me, even when her mother used to pick on me, threatening to break my legs. She took me to the room next door, and I was speechless: my father was on the wall, looking back at me. It was his picture, the very same photograph I'd cut out, but this one was almost life-size.

I stood there all afternoon, and finally, at some point in the early evening, Ahmad came to see me: "Hi, Zarifa, *Eid Mubarak!*"

"Eid Mubarak, Ahmad jan. Where does this picture come from? I have often asked you for a picture of him, but you always said you didn't have any!"

"Yes, I found it and had it enlarged about two weeks ago," he replied.

Ahmad had been only eighteen years old when our father passed away. As the eldest, he then became responsible for his younger brothers and sisters. The memories were very painful for him, too. I took a picture of the portrait using his smartphone and emailed it to myself. I lay down on the *toshaks* and stared at him. My father . . . I tried to read his expression and looked for similarities between us. I would have loved to be able to hug him.

A few days later, my mother was browsing my Facebook page on her phone like she often did—was it out of curiosity or distrust? She commented on my pictures one by one, with a detached expression, until she stumbled upon the photo of my father. Her face tensed.

"What is he doing there?" she asked.

She turned off her phone and walked away. I then hurried to hide the precious memory I had briefly chosen as a profile picture on Facebook. But I was at peace. I had finally looked my father in the eye, and I had seen myself in his gaze.

Was all this a sign? Right after the Eid celebrations, I received some good news. A call, followed by an email, informed me that I had passed the first round of entrance exams for the university in Kabul. I still had to take the oral exams. I had to devote all my energy to preparing. Here was my chance, within reach.

Failing was simply not an option.

9

GETTING TO UNIVERSITY

"And how do you see your future?"

"Above all, I want to live."

The oral exam I had to pass to get into university in Bishkek took place at the American Embassy in Kabul, a giant, well-guarded, and intimidating compound. A person needed an appointment to enter, and was allowed in only after being thoroughly searched. During the exam, two American women took turns asking me questions. Although they were friendly and smiled a lot, their tone was serious. I had warned them when I sat down: "I'm nervous. This is one of the most important days of my life."

The interview continued with generalities, then all of a sudden, they said: "Tell us a bit more about yourself. Why do you think you deserve the scholarship?"

I then mustered all my conviction and charm and told them my story: the challenges I had faced in order to be able to study, the trips back and forth to Pakistan, the war, the Taliban, the fact I had to work at the same time . . . I was so tense, I didn't even think to mention straightaway my English course in Turkey or the program at Yale, or even the concert in Davos—ridiculous!

They listened to me kindly, and when I started talking about the Zohra Orchestra, they immediately brought up Davos. This relaxed me right away. I felt completely comfortable telling them about my passions and ambitions in life: "I want to be independent, obtain a master's degree, and, afterward, get a PhD from Harvard. I want to write books, lots of books, and to help children, specifically girls, achieve their dreams. But, above all, I want to be happy."

The interview lasted at least a half hour, twice as long as the other candidates' interviews. The tone remained focused and respectful, but before I stood up to leave, both women smiled sincerely at me and wished me good luck. I came out feeling confident, telling myself: *It'll work out. At least someone seems to like the "bad girl"!*

Soon after that, the second piece of good news arrived: I had gotten into the American university in Kabul! For that oral exam, I had been interviewed by a young Afghan graduate who'd worn a satisfied look on his face and not asked many questions. The main thing he'd explained to me was that the scholarship would only cover 85 percent of the fees if I got in. In short, the interview had been a bit quick, rushed even.

Kabul, that was already something, right?! I was going to be able to start my higher education! That was all true. But I wanted more than ever now to leave, to get away from my family and from Afghanistan, to rid myself of my city as if it were a heavy, burdensome cloak. I had to make too many concessions here, had too many roles to play. Plus, that summer had been particularly difficult, due to the repeated attacks that were occurring in Kabul. A climate of fear hung over the city. Enormous explosions reverberated through the air almost every afternoon. After each one, a black pillar of smoke filled with fragments of debris and dust would rise up into the sky.

Our neighborhood was frequently the target of such attacks—was it ISIS or the Taliban that was behind them? No one ever knew. They all hated the Hazaras equally. During one of these attacks, a car bomb exploded and destroyed Kabul's center for wrestling—a very popular sport.

I was right nearby when it happened. I could feel the bomb's blast as strongly as if someone had punched me in the stomach and knocked the wind out of me. Shock, then chaos, screaming . . . The windows shattered all around us. I was so scared that I threw myself, shaking, into a taxi to get home. Mom, who had seen images of the attack on TV, was in a panic, convinced I had been killed. The cell phone networks were, of course, overwhelmed after every attack. Everyone would feverishly try to reach their loved ones, especially if the attack had happened during rush hour, when people were traveling to or from the office or school, and when the streets were crowded.

Protests had erupted all over the city, and the anger was rising. People said, "This government is incapable of protecting us." Young Hazaras formed a people's militia and patrolled Shiite neighborhoods, trying to detect potential suicide bombers. One day, as I was being driven home from the radio station, a patrol stopped my cab, forced me out, and beat up the poor driver, a Pashtun. They chased him away as they threatened him: "We don't want to see you pick up any more Hazara girls! Get out of here!"

Then they took me home, gripping me tightly: "We know where you live. If we see you hanging out with a Pashtun again, we'll kill him."

I was terrified. The bigotry clearly went both ways. For several days, my brother Ali escorted me to a shared taxi outside the neighborhood so I could escape undetected.

It was during this period of violence and tension that I went to Sri Lanka for a couple of days, thanks to my friends at the ArtLords. Innovation for Change, an international program that supports civil rights and promotes awareness in young people, had organized a three-day workshop in Colombo on the theme "Arts Lab for Social Change." They had invited about thirty young activists from eight different Asian countries to participate. Naturally, I applied as soon as I saw their ad on Facebook, even before Omaid, the president of ArtLords, who was involved in the event as an Afghan representative, suggested I take part.

Five young people had been selected to represent Afghanistan at the roundtables, three boys and two girls: Khandan and me. Both of us were Hazara, and, incidentally, we were seated in economy class, while the boys traveled in business class.

In this way, we left with Omaid and Lala Kabir and spent three dreamlike days in Sri Lanka. During this trip, I really got to know Kabir. This was something that would be valuable to me in the upcoming months.

As per usual, I barely made it to the airport in time. At home, nobody had tried to stop me from traveling, but as always, a certain nervous anxiety accompanied our embraces and goodbyes. On top of it all, it was Massoud Day: the anniversary of the death of Ahmad Shah Massoud, the leader of the Afghan mujahideen who had resisted the Soviets and the Taliban and who'd been assassinated on September 9, 2001, two days before the 9/11 attacks in the United States. Numerous roads were blocked, and I was the last one to join the group. Strangely, I didn't feel as excited as I usually did to get on the plane.

I had barely done any research about Sri Lanka before the trip; my mind had been elsewhere—I was practically at university already or, in any case, waiting for the verdict regarding Bishkek. So, what a delightful surprise it was to discover Colombo!

We were driven to a magnificent hotel on the seafront. We didn't see anything on the way there since we'd arrived at night, but the driver was so welcoming and even respected all the red lights! This immediately relaxed me and made me feel safe after the chaos of Kabul. I knew I was going to love this trip. My room, complete with its own fruit basket on the table, seemed incredibly luxurious to me. I went to bed and fell instantly asleep. How long had it been since I'd slept so well?

With no fear of attacks, militias, financial troubles, or family tensions and no anxiety regarding my future.

When I woke up at dawn, I rushed to the balcony and felt the ocean's breeze on my face. I ran to the beach, and simply seeing the sea and hearing the waves again moved me to tears—I felt strangled with happiness. Just like on my trip to Turkey a few years before, on that beach in Antalya, it felt like the sea was washing away my problems, my worries, and my stress. The experience filled me with hope and energy. I was so happy to be there. Once again, I promised myself that one day, I would bring my mother, my brothers, and sister to the sea. Then I went back to the hotel for breakfast.

In the hall and dining room, I met young people from Sri Lanka, India, Pakistan—from all over—who were there representing their projects and organizations. On the first day, the ArtLords introduced their work: explaining the precautions they had to take when painting, what it meant to stand up against the corrupt elites and armed rebels in a war-torn city, the threats they were facing. Then the discussion opened up. I had been invited as a musician to join a panel about the role art could play in young people's lives.

Omaid and I sat down next to an Indian rapper and activist. She was insufferable and kept trying to snatch the microphone out of my hands. A moderator asked us about our work: how we learned, rehearsed; if we were able to give concerts; what we thought we could bring to society; and how we saw ourselves enacting change in our respective countries.

I explained to the delegates in front of me that an all-female orchestra, conducted by a girl, performing outside of Afghanistan in front of an international audience—in Davos, no less—that played both traditional Afghan music and classics from the Western canon, was the best image we could offer of our country. No political leader could say or do as much, as Omaid had pointed out to me when we'd first met. I remembered how strong and powerful I had felt in Davos, as if I were speaking to the whole world.

Among the people who impressed me during this trip was a group of transgender activists. Being around them further strengthened my conviction to fight for human rights. They faced such terrible difficulties.

Aisha, who was Pakistani, told us what she had gone through in her family—who no longer spoke to her—and in society. Mockery, exclusion, discrimination . . . Members of the trans community were often associated with begging and prostitution. Sometimes in my own life, I felt like a burden, like I didn't matter, like nobody cared. But Aisha was a real hero. At twenty-eight, she was teaching at university and fighting to pass a law recognizing equal rights for trans people, despite the extremist forces that were working against them. What a strange country.

A person only lives once. In my mind, those who were making the most of their lives were those among us who were doing something, who were fighting and struggling, for themselves or for people who suffered.

Those three days passed by very quickly. The weather was nice; we laughed, we worked, we talked. The food was delicious, and I often went to the beach. We spent one whole night drinking green tea and singing with Omaid, Lala Kabir, and Rayed.

Originally from Kapisa, Rayed had joined ArtLords as a project manager while studying at university. He'd quickly become my friend. After our first encounter, the ArtLords had suggested I join them, and I visited their workshop as often as I could and sometimes helped them with small tasks. Whenever I was with these men, it was as if we had always known each other!

Lala Kabir sang a very beautiful Afghan song by the singer Ahmad Zahir. Then Omaid talked to me as if he were my older brother. I told him about an idea I had for a book that was starting to take shape, this book.

"I want to talk about us Afghan girls. I want to tell my story, how I found music and how it changed my life. But I'm hesitant. What will my mother think? What will my family say? I'm afraid of hurting everyone; I'm afraid they will disown me and cut all ties."

It was true, I couldn't seem to make up my mind. One day, I wanted to say everything, expose everything. The next day, I wanted to give up, hide it all.

"Stop being so afraid, Zarifa," Omaid urged me that evening. "You just need to learn how to control your anxiety. Concentrate and go for it. Sometimes you'll feel like you've hit rock bottom, but you know that every time you do, you'll get back on top. You've been through this before—the seemingly hopeless moments, the discouragement—but you're much stronger than you think."

During this euphoric interlude in Colombo, I was checking my emails one morning when I immediately noticed I had received one from the AUCA, titled "Application Status." It was news that could change my life forever. Trembling, I opened the email:

> Dear applicant,
>
> I am pleased to inform you that you have been selected by the State Department, through the U.S. Embassy in Afghanistan, to receive a full scholarship to join the preparatory class of 2018-2019 at the American University of Central Asia [. . .] We would like to congratulate you and your family.
>
> Year after year, we are honored to welcome the young leaders of tomorrow and hope that you will soon become a distinguished representative of the AUCA.

The email was signed by the coordinator of the Afghan student program in Bishkek, Kyrgyzstan: Ekaterina, my future guardian angel.

She suggested I visit the university's website. The date was September 12, 2018. I would leave home in October, after obtaining my visa for Kyrgyzstan.

"Yesssssss! I got in! I'm going to leave Kabul!"

I was so happy, I probably woke up the entire hotel that morning. I felt dizzy, ecstatic, relieved. I had butterflies in my stomach.

I will finally be able to fulfill my dream, to shed all the constraints weighing down on me in Afghanistan, to be myself. But I will be alone, I don't know anyone there. Plus, will my family even let me go, leave the house and the country? Will my mother accept my departure? How will she manage without me?

I sprinted down the hotel corridor at full speed, caught the elevator, and ran to tell my friends the news. As they had been so many times before, Omaid and Lala Kabir were there to congratulate me, encourage me, soothe my fears, and rejoice with me. That evening, we drank tea, laughed, and sang to celebrate my success.

To be on the safe side, I decided not to tell my mother yet. I preferred to inform her in person I was leaving: only after I had received both the visa and plane ticket, thus backing her into a corner—or in this case, an airport gangway. My strategy was to present her with a fait accompli.

Deep down, though, I knew that no matter what happened, I was going to leave. I didn't have the slightest intention of giving up. In the meantime, I continued working at the radio station and with the ArtLords. I kept a low profile. But in my mind, everything was suddenly speeding up. My life had finally shifted up a gear.

After I returned from Colombo, I was invited to the American University of Kabul's orientation. I wasn't sure what to do. I had to confirm my registration soon, but if I turned down my spot at the university in Kabul and something went wrong with the scholarship or my visa for Bishkek, I'd lose everything. I'd be back to square one. My friends advised me to be careful. Even those who thought, like I did, that it would be best if I left the country for a while suggested I secure my spot in Kabul anyway.

They were right, and so that's what I did. I showed up for the two-day-long orientation sessions that were designed to put new students at ease and explain the university system and course outlines to them. All of us had put on our smartest outfits and were trying to show ourselves in the best possible light. I was wearing a green T-shirt and blue pants. I had tied back my hair and fastened my headscarf around my neck—with the sides crossed and thrown back, as usual.

I already knew many of the students on campus, some of whom had even become my friends during our English course in Turkey. Current students gave us welcome packages that contained a backpack with the AUAF logo, notebooks, and pens, and they also assisted the teachers with the orientation. The administration greeted us with a welcome speech and showed a video presenting the university and its curriculum. All of this was interspersed with small snack breaks. On the second day, they organized icebreaker games, and both boys and girls participated and laughed together.

As I contemplated this scene, I thought about the attack the Taliban had made on this haven of freedom a little more than two years before, on August 24, 2016, and could imagine their hatred. The Taliban had invaded the campus in the late afternoon, and the horror had lasted for several hours. They had wanted there to be as many victims as possible.

First, the terrorists had forced their way in through an adjacent school. Then they had occupied the various floors of the university building, searching the classrooms one by one and shooting point-blank at students, both boys and girls, who were begging for mercy and trying to escape the bullets. Parents waited outside the campus gates all night to receive news of their children—and, in some cases, to claim their bodies.

According to the official count, sixteen students were killed and dozens more injured in the attack. A friend of mine, Sami Sarwari, was among the victims. At the ANIM, Sami had played the *dilruba*—a string instrument from India whose name literally translates to "enchanting the heart"—and he had just made a brilliant start to his studies at the university. Some of the injured remain paralyzed to this day; they had thrown themselves out the window to avoid being shot.

A month after that attack, two teachers, an Australian and an American, were kidnapped as they left campus. The Taliban kept them hostage for more than three years before finally releasing them in a prisoner exchange. After these tragic events, the AUAF's security precautions were rigorously reinforced with blast-proof walls that surrounded the compound. To get inside, a person had to prove their credentials, and, as a further precaution, foreign teachers residing on campus were no longer allowed to leave the compound for the entirety of their stay.

But the memories of these tragedies faded as I entered the premises. Inside, I was dazzled by the classrooms and meeting rooms, the library, the students walking by with their books under their arms, chatting with the professors. I knew that if I were to stay there, I would definitely be happy. But I still hoped to leave the country. It was taking a while to hear back from Bishkek—the American Embassy was waiting for the go-ahead (and funds) from Washington. I was told that the Trump administration had reduced the scope of their international cooperation, and so the total sum of scholarships granted—particularly to young Afghans—had also been reduced. But my faith remained unshaken as I discreetly prepared for my departure.

In the end, I received a new email from Ekaterina confirming my scholarship and my admission to the university in Bishkek on the last day of orientation in Kabul. I left the orientation immediately. My choice had already been made. I told the AUAF that I wouldn't take up my place, as I had been admitted to university elsewhere. Other young people were on the waiting list, and it was only fair that I gave up my spot as soon as possible.

Then my plane ticket and visa finally arrived. It was recommended that students bring warm clothes and snow boots. I couldn't put it off any longer—I had to talk to Mom. She'd obviously realized something was up, but without knowing what it actually was, what could she think was happening? But, as soon as I opened my mouth, I could see from her expression that she had known this moment would come. She wasn't really surprised, merely curious.

It was dinnertime, and we had gathered on the *toshaks* in the living room with my brothers and my sister, a dish of rice between us. I took a deep breath.

"I have something to tell you."

I announced that in one week, I would be gone. Without even waiting for our mother to react, Ali said he was thrilled for me. Najla was incredibly hyper as she reacted. "Sweet! Now I'm sure I can leave, too, no one can stop me! Thank you, Zarifa! Thank you! Thank you!" she exclaimed, almost dancing with joy.

After all, it was up to the firstborn to lead the way!

My mother was unequivocal at first: "You're not going!" I was expecting this reaction. She seemed to be worried mainly about the money. "Who will work if you leave? How will we manage without you?"

"I'll work!" Ali answered immediately.

"Why don't you stay here? Study and work here? This is your home . . . ," Mom tried.

Then she tried again to object, knowing full well that nothing—not even she—could stop me: "Someone in my family told me her daughter had gotten a scholarship to study, but her father didn't let her go. They said girls had to stay at home so their parents could keep an eye on them. And anyway, it isn't good for girls to go abroad. It's not safe. You can't do that sort of thing."

Of course, I had already traveled abroad to Turkey, Yale, and Europe for the tour. I had always managed to convince her. But this time, the situation was different. I would be gone for a long time. She probably sensed this, and I'm sure that she knew I would leave anyway. In the end, she didn't really put up a fight. Rather, I had the impression she was just thinking out loud and was actually happy that I had the opportunity to go to university. That evening, she was undoubtedly a bit confused, feeling a little lost or worried, but also happy and proud.

Over the next couple of days, as was her custom, she changed her mind several times. Why didn't I just stay at the university in Kabul if I had been admitted? Sonia, a French friend of mine who was a journalist and spoke Dari, drove me home one Friday after an afternoon of shopping for my departure to Bishkek. She took the opportunity to talk to my mother:

"You should be proud, you know. When Zarifa comes back, she will surely find a good job. She could work for the government or maybe even the UN. You have to let her go, Anis Gul. It's the chance of a lifetime."

That settled it. Mom really liked Sonia. She trusted her. She had seen how she worked hard, alone, far from her country and her family, and this had earned Mom's respect. And, the UN, really? Could a mother dream of any work more prestigious for her daughter? My mother, siblings, and I, however, tacitly agreed not to tell anyone else in our inner circle yet, neither the family nor the neighbors. There would always be time enough to explain later. I spent my last couple of days saying goodbye to my friends, feeling excited and tense.

The Afghan students who were leaving at the same time created a Facebook group so we could get to know each other. There were eight girls and two boys—this was the year of *girl power*! Evidently this upset a couple of the unsuccessful male candidates who thought they were much better than us. Some girls in the group were worried about the meager eighty-pound luggage limit! *How funny*, I thought. I had packed all my things—I really thought I had brought everything

I needed—and mine barely weighed forty pounds. What on earth did they have in their bags?!

I had the feeling that this was just the first of many things that would astonish me, and that from then on, I would be going from one surprise to another. After all, that's what I had been waiting for all this time!

Now, more than ever, I was ready and open to adventure.

10

A STUDENT IN BISHKEK!

We arrived in Bishkek, the capital of Kyrgyzstan, on a cold, rainy morning in October 2018. It was still dark outside. I had been similarly greeted by the rain a couple of years before on the Turkish coast, in Antalya. Our guide then had assured us that this was a positive sign for travelers. So, this time, I saw it as a good omen, too, and I was not mistaken. Indeed, little did I know how right I was.

The day before, all the successful Afghan candidates had met up at the airport in Kabul. After taking a couple of pictures and hugging our families goodbye, we boarded the plane that would take us to Bishkek via Dubai. I had waited until the very last moment to inform the family of my departure. A few hours before I was due to board, Mom had invited everyone over for dinner: my big brother Ahmad and his family, my older sisters, the Uncles. Ahmad was the first to show his concern. I think he was a bit overwhelmed but not angry.

I knew that when it came right down to it, this new phase of my life would only confirm their suspicions. I was a "bad girl." An outsider. Different, at best. But I couldn't change that. I was definitely never going to be like the others.

As for Mom, she was positively glowing with pride. To my surprise, and regardless of whatever they might have thought of me and said behind my back, everyone was in a good mood that night and the dinner went really well. Were they happy to see me go? Relieved, maybe . . . But I was already elsewhere. I was standing at the precipice of a new life, and I was nervous. I couldn't swallow the *ashaks*—Afghan dumplings—or any of the other food we had spent the whole afternoon preparing.

I was starving the following morning when we arrived in Bishkek. Thankfully, despite the early start, Ekaterina came to meet us at the airport. She'd thought of everything. She welcomed us warmly and handed out bananas and water before inviting us to board a minibus.

As the sun began to rise, I contemplated my new home. In some ways, Bishkek didn't seem to be very different from Kabul—it was another stop on the Silk Road—but here, there were no barricades, no military checkpoints, and, most importantly, no terrorist attacks! Like Kabul, the Kyrgyz capital was surrounded by snowy peaks and boasted traditional bazaars and winding alleys, as well as wide avenues lined with imposing buildings—a legacy from the time when the country belonged to the former USSR. The Soviet administration had sent a number of Russians to live in the city before the USSR's collapse, and many Russians still remained here.

Less than thirty minutes later, after passing birch forests and green parks, Ekaterina accompanied us to the university dormitories. That first year, I would share a big room with two Kyrgyz girls. Students at Bishkek came from all over Central Asia—Kazakhstan, Tajikistan, Turkmenistan, Afghanistan, and Kyrgyzstan, of course—and the university encouraged us all to mingle. Each of us had a bed, a wardrobe, and a desk. I had more privacy here than I'd ever had at home, and I felt reassured to learn that I wouldn't be alone.

Above my desk, I stuck a few pictures of Mom and the kids, a drawing by the ArtLords, some sheet music, and three Post-its that I would look at every day to remind myself of what was important:

1. I AM HERE SO I CAN GO TO HARVARD ONE DAY.
2. LEARN TO LOVE YOURSELF—stop relying on others.
3. LIVE YOUR LIFE—you only live once.

On my desk, I placed my favorite books, including *Becoming*, Michelle Obama's autobiography, which had just come out that fall, as well as my new journal, titled *Only Zarifa*. Reading the former first lady's book, I had been touched to discover that she had learned to play the piano as a child. Most importantly, I realized that she had always known who she wanted to be and had devoted herself to her studies to make it happen. As a young Black girl, she'd had to fight hard to forge her way forward, starting when she was a teenager. It also became clear to me as I read that Barack Obama would have never become president without her. Who could be a better role model?

I began exploring Bishkek the next day. The city wasn't much prettier than Kabul, but it was clean and calm. The biggest difference was that everyone in Bishkek, including the girls, wandered freely around the streets, even at night. During the day, I walked around with a smile on my face, and in the evening, I went running with my headphones on. I could wear whatever I wanted. People dressed for the weather and according to their own tastes. There was no need for a woman to cover her hair or wear long-sleeved tops or ankle-length dresses unless she chose to do so. Some women did; the old women from the countryside who sold fruit on the city center's sidewalks were easily identifiable by their beautiful headscarves, which they wore knotted at the back of their heads. I didn't hear any nasty remarks about women. None of us were harassed or threatened.

I became enthralled by the campus the very first time I visited it. It was modern with large lawns where we students would meet up on sunny days and hang out between classes. And inside the main building there was a sort of atrium with concrete stands where we gathered on the first day for our orientation. The classrooms were all situated around the atrium, and there were small canteens on every floor, some of them open to a terrace that overlooked the mountains. And let's not forget the free Wi-Fi. Everything was friendly, new, and welcoming—particularly the library, which had thousands of books printed in English. The student life I had dreamed of for so long was going to start here!

Of the small group of new Afghan students, I was at first the only one who'd taken off her headscarf since leaving Kabul. The others were still wearing them on the first day of university. But eventually, over the first couple of weeks, most of the others took theirs off, too. Soon enough, they didn't even want to look at the pictures we took the day we left Kabul! Those among us who kept their headscarves on did so by choice.

Most of my female friends who had been in Bishkek for several years—Afghans and foreigners alike—would wear skirts that ended above the knees, minidresses, and shorts when it was hot. I bought myself a pair of shorts, too, one day when I was feeling particularly bold. Five times, I put them on while I was at home, but I was unable to bring myself to go out dressed like that.

My life in Bishkek, especially during those first couple of months, was filled with discovery and trying new things. As I got to know other students—Kyrgyz, Tajik, Kazakh, Uzbek—I came to realize that my country was by far the most conservative in the region. As I grasped how deeply the war and the Taliban had influenced our ways of life and ways of thinking, I felt even more angry at them for having sent us back into the past. I also noticed that the Afghan boys struggled more than the girls to get used to this new environment, at least in the beginning. They kept to themselves and huddled together like baby chicks, criticizing those of us they considered to be "too liberated," as if our behavior was a betrayal of our country.

"I don't think you have to renounce your culture and traditions just because you study abroad."

That's how the conversation started in the university cafeteria. The boy who had spoken was from Kandahar, and he belonged to the group of students who had been particularly irritated by the fact the scholarship recipients were mostly female. Fayaz had passed on many of the unpleasant comments made by the unsuccessful candidates, those who claimed they had done "so much better" than the selected girls. He always looked at students who wore jeans and tennis shoes, and the girls who went bare-legged, with contempt. And, of course, this comment was also an indirect dig at me. I couldn't let him get away with it, even if we got along quite well otherwise.

"It's got nothing to do with culture and traditions, Fayaz. I love my country and respect Allah, but I see no reason to cover my hair!"

If our outfits shocked him, he certainly was unprepared for what he had coming in philosophy class! I loved following in the footsteps of the great Greek thinkers: Socrates, Plato, and many others. The class was such a mind-opening experience for all of us. When we studied Mary Wollstonecraft or Aristophanes's *Lysistrata* or the Bhagavad Gita, we had debates about sex, religion, and race—things we would not ordinarily discuss openly. We were encouraged to have our own opinions and question every word in all the literature we read.

One day, the teacher, who had assigned us the *Epic of Gilgamesh*— one of the oldest texts known to humankind—asked us students to define the difference between "gender" and "sex." It was a provocative question and made certain students, especially the Afghans, extremely uncomfortable. Some of the boys jumped in, trying to define "gender" by the presence or absence of "certain body parts," but wouldn't name which parts they were referring to. Silently the teacher picked up a piece of chalk and wrote on the blackboard, *Penis, vagina* . . . He then turned around to face us.

"We are here to study. When you express yourselves in an academic context, you must use precise vocabulary, even when it comes to naming body parts. Nose, arm, foot . . . Boys, I guess it isn't too difficult for you to say the word 'penis.' But what about 'vagina'? Go on, Hikmat, it's your turn."

The poor boy went for it. "Vagina . . . ," he whispered, barely able to spit out the last syllable.

"Louder!" insisted the teacher.

Eventually, the unfortunate Hikmat did as he was told, his face scarlet with embarrassment.

This story still makes me laugh when I tell it! It illustrates the huge cultural gulf that existed between us and our professors, a gulf they aimed to bridge during our time with them at university. They helped to free us from the stereotypes and obsessive taboos that were prevalent in our societies, to rid ourselves of the shame so frequently associated with our bodies. Once again, I noticed that the girls dealt with the situation better than the boys. Perhaps it was because we felt the pressing need for change and progress much more acutely than the boys did.

The first year of university was an adjustment period, but also an opportunity for people to catch up in the fundamental courses: math; written English; and also Russian, the official language of Kyrgyzstan. This transition period at the New Generation Academy (NGA) would prepare us for the American university curriculum we would start the following year.

During those first seven months, I also discovered my weaknesses. I really struggled in math. I'd always known I wasn't that good, but the situation turned out to be a lot worse than I thought! In truth, my inconsistent schooling meant that I had never really studied mathematics properly. I was ignorant. The subject seemed to come so effortlessly to the others—when they would discuss things like physics or chemistry, most of the time I had no idea what they were talking about. So,

I made the most of my Wi-Fi access to do as much research as I could online.

In the end, my cramming paid off, and I passed the class even if I never grew to love math. I also took the opportunity to warn my brothers and sister that they really had to study and make an effort in this subject.

I struggled even more with Russian. I now had to master yet another new alphabet, different again from Persian, Urdu, and English. But I always tried to use the language wherever I could. This often made people laugh at me in shops. Soon enough, though, I was able to make myself understood.

At first, I thought that these preparatory classes were unnecessary. I was already twenty years old and would have preferred to start my university studies right away. But in hindsight, I understood how much I needed this year of transition. It was crucial not only academically but also mentally and psychologically, and it helped me to calm down, adjust, and find my footing.

I managed to get a job at an English language center, where I taught a few hours a week, although every hour-long class meant long rides in an overcrowded minibus there and back. I also saved money from my scholarship. In this way, I managed each month to send nearly two hundred dollars to Mom. I still felt a little guilty about leaving her and my siblings behind.

At the same time, I felt the urge to finally live like other girls my age. My peers had come to Bishkek with the support of their parents. Some of them were rich; others had scholarships like me. But none of them had to worry about whether their relatives would be able to eat or stay warm. They were able to completely devote themselves to their studies without asking themselves too many questions—except, of course, during those times when we got news of yet another attack back home.

Within the first few months, one girl learned of her father's death right in the middle of class. Of course, we felt sorry for her and supported her as much as we could. But I have to admit that, in a way, I almost envied her grief. I know this is a horrible thing to say, but she at least had known the father she was mourning. She had loved him and been loved in return. Listening to my new friends talk about their childhoods, families, houses, and good memories made it clearer than ever to me just how little joy there had been in my life. Sometimes, it felt like my resentment was too much to bear. I was angry at the world and everyone in it.

In those moments when I was consumed by dark thoughts, which often happened on weekends and at night, I would call Lala Kabir. He had become one of my closest confidants. He would listen to me patiently, motivate me, advise me. He insisted it was time for me to move on, to let go of my anger and put it aside, so I could "live my life," just as I had said I would do when I took the oral exam to get here. I had said that I intended to live the life, dream the dreams, and pursue the ambitions of a normal twenty-year-old girl.

Lala Kabir had already warned me, in Colombo, that I must stop dwelling on my past. "You are here, but because your mind is still with your family in Kabul, you're missing out on the good things life has to offer."

During the winter holidays, the campus was completely empty. My friends either went home to see their parents or went skiing outside Bishkek. Having no money whatsoever, I was the only one who remained on campus. It snowed a lot. Both the university and the library were closed, and I felt incredibly alone in the deserted dormitory.

I barely had the means to go out for coffee, but I had plenty of time for introspection. I spent three days thinking, turning over in my mind the advice Lala Kabir had given me. He was right. His words kept playing in my head, over and over again. I called him and confided in him once more, and he was immediately encouraging: "Go on, Zarifa. Talk to her. Talk to your mother."

That was easier said than done. I started by tidying up my room while I thought things through. I felt like I was also tidying up my brain, my life, by sweeping away the past, clearing up the present, and preparing for the future.

It was early evening on January 1—the first day of a new year. It was already dark outside, and all was quiet. I sat down in front of my computer. My hands were sweaty, and my stomach was in knots. I eventually opened up Skype and called her.

"Mom? How are you?"

At first, I talked about everything and nothing. Finally, I mustered all my courage and said, "Are you home alone? Are you free for the next thirty minutes? I have a couple of things I need to talk to you about."

I now believe that my mother had also wanted to speak to me for quite some time. But neither of us had really had the opportunity or strength to do so. I remember exactly what I said to her that day. It felt like someone was ripping my heart out of my chest, but I couldn't keep it all inside any longer, and I sensed a new energy pulsing through me, driving me to do it. The urge was so powerful it took my breath away.

"Mom, I'm sick of having to work, sick of teaching these classes so far away from campus. I'm going to stop. I'm tired, and it's affecting my studies. I need to devote all my time to school, especially math and Russian, if I want to succeed. I'll send you what money I can, but it won't come every month, or even on a regular basis."

"Okay, okay . . . What's going on? Why are you saying all this?"

"Look, there are many things that have been on my mind over the last few years, even since childhood, to be honest . . . I think it's time we talk about it, and I know you have things to tell me, too."

"Okay . . ." She would only answer in monosyllables, in a few words at most. She was visibly confused and a little tense.

"Mom, do you remember that day after I came back from Davos, when we decided to go to Pakistan, and you called Dad to explain that it would be safer for me there? Do you remember that night?"

"No . . . But go on."

"You had a fight. I heard him say: 'Take your daughter with you but don't touch my children.' You were so mad at me that you threw the phone on the floor and shouted: 'This is all because of you!'"

Silence.

"And it wasn't just that night. I've felt this way so many times and for so long. You have repeatedly told me or made me feel like I was a problem, *your* problem. Whenever you got angry at something or someone, you would often blame me for it. You would yell: 'It's all your fault.' You never thought about how much it hurt me to hear you say that.

"I was able to put up with everything else. Waking up at five in the morning while everyone was still asleep to teach classes, cleaning up the house alone, watching you take the boys out to dinner, walking for two hours to the ANIM with shoes full of holes because I didn't have enough money for the bus. At the end of the day, none of that mattered. Even when you sent me to my brother Ahmad's house, and I had to stop going to school and was treated like a housekeeper by his wife. Even that didn't upset me as much as that night, remember? The night Basir told you to take *your* daughter but forbade you from taking *his* children to Quetta. And you said to me: 'Just disappear!' You couldn't bear to look at me. He rejected me, and instead of defending me, you kicked me out . . ."

I kept talking, I didn't cry. There was silence on the other end of the line. "And when I explained to you that it wasn't fair that I was the only one who had to earn a living, and you retorted, 'Oh, now that you're making money, you think you can talk to me like that?'"

I went on. I was finally getting everything off my chest.

"I never asked you about my father because I didn't want to hurt you, but you never gave me the chance to get to know him. I want you to tell me about him."

She remained silent. Not once did she try to interrupt me. As prideful as she was, she did not utter a word. She kept everything she was thinking and feeling inside.

Where did I find the courage and strength to tell her all this? I was twenty years old, and all alone in Bishkek. But I think the change of scenery and the distance helped.

I wasn't finished.

"At the same time, Mom, I know that everything I will achieve in my life will be because of you or, rather, thanks to you. Everything that I am and everything that I will become. Because when it comes down to it, you've always been there for me. You let me go to school. And after abandoning me at Ahmad's, you came back to get me. If I had stayed there, I would surely be married by now with three or four children. So, I also want to thank you. Thank you for all you've done for me. You mean everything to me."

I had never expressed all these thoughts aloud, especially those words of thanks. I don't think I've ever been as close to her as I was that night. For years, there had been so much anger, so much left unsaid between us.

Pouring out one's heart like this was not something we usually did in our family. But at that moment, I lost control and burst into tears as I explained how important it was to me to be able to tell her all these things.

"Good. Maybe one day we'll talk about this again . . . ," she replied gently.

But I knew what she meant by "maybe"—I sensed immediately we would never return to the subject. Perhaps she would never even speak to me again?

"Okay, Mom, we'll talk about it some other time." Suddenly, I felt terrified of losing her. I hung up and went to bed, although I was incapable of sleep.

The next morning, as soon as I woke up, I sent a message to Lala Kabir: "I did it. I called my mother. She didn't say anything. All she said is we would maybe talk about it later. But I think it's over. She will never call me back. I have nobody left."

I didn't feel any better. I certainly didn't feel any freer than before.

Yet a couple of days later, she reached out to me. But her tone was completely different. This time, my mother was the one who cried.

"Zarifa, you're right. About everything. But let me tell you something, I have never felt this close to any of my other children. I have five children, and they're like the five fingers of my hand. If I were to lose one of them, the pain would destroy me. I love all my children equally, and think you are each special in your own way. Perhaps it's because you're my eldest, because you were the one who had to help me, that you were the one I yelled at the most. But it's also true that you were the only one I could always count on, that I could confide in. I never cared about you any less than the others, even though I may have treated you differently."

Then she assured me that she had loved me from the day I was born. "Oh, I love you, too, so very much," I replied.

It was the first time we had said "I love you" to each other. We talked about the past again, about the state I'd been in when I came back from Ahmad's, about the courage it took her to come get me, to resist the family's pressure.

Sometime after that conversation, Mom told me that she had enrolled herself in school. She said she wanted to learn how to read and write, too, since she'd never had the opportunity before. I'm certain she had been thinking about doing this for a while. I wonder if, in addition to me leaving for university, our conversation had convinced her, or at least helped motivate her, to do it. It was time for her to finally achieve her own independence as well. Neither she, nor anyone at home, believed that Basir would ever obtain an Australian visa. The wise decision would have been for him to return to Kabul to take care of his family, but he did not. It was a question of honor for him. But what honor could he have believed there to be in abandoning his wife and children in one of the most dangerous cities in the world?

Regardless of what Basir planned to do, I was thrilled by my mother's decision. I was overjoyed, and so proud of her! My mother, despite her fears and prejudices, had always believed in herself, and now she also believed in her chances of achieving something of her own. Just like Ali and Najla, who could also picture themselves studying at university one day.

I was happy to think that I had fulfilled my duty as the firstborn. I was paving the way.

11

A NEW LIFE

I could now do things that would have been unthinkable in my previous life: stroll around, light and carefree, exploring the avenues of Bishkek lined with birch trees. It felt much like the moment I had removed my headscarf at the beach in Antalya to feel the wind in my hair fully. Here, for the first time, I could read in cafés, try horseback riding, and go for a run at dawn or a walk in the evening. Ever since my arrival, I had gone from one discovery to another. Bishkek made me feel good—it had become my city. I had never known that moving to another country would lead me to experience so many new, albeit simple, pleasures. I had only imagined that it might, and hoped against hope that this would happen for me one day.

The first few weeks at university, the other female students—those who eventually became dear friends—would poke gentle fun at me. They called me "auntie" because of my bare face, devoid of makeup, and my habit of dressing like their frumpy female relatives straight from the provinces. I had thought my leggings and pink tennis shoes were rebellious and brazen, but here I bumped into girls in minidresses, with bare arms and high heels, wearing eye shadow and lipstick.

In Bishkek, my new friends were my age. This was a departure from my last year in Kabul, when most of my friends had been older than me. I had kept in touch with the ANIM gang, of course, but between our busy schedules and the attacks that limited how much we could travel, we had seen each other less and less. And I had also understood that we were taking different paths in life.

Now at university, everything was simpler, and I was able to spend more time with my peers. In the evenings, at the café, or between classes, we shared our stories and our lives. Some students, especially the Afghan girls, had also had difficult pasts, like me. I found this out as we slowly began opening up and trusting one another. After everything we'd gone through, it was good for us to know that others had suffered from shame and fear, too. We were able to listen and support each other in our dreams for the future. Where would we be in twenty years? Here at the university, girls could breathe.

One of them told me she had been married off to a man she didn't know. Afterward, he had left her alone in Afghanistan with her mother-in-law while he went to Europe for work. Her mother-in-law treated the girl so badly that she ended up seeking refuge with her parents, who gave her permission to leave. She felt safe here at university but still feared retaliation from her husband, who categorically refused to divorce her. Another girl, who dreamed of becoming an engineer, dreaded returning to her family for the upcoming summer holidays. What if they didn't let her come back? Her mother had started talking about marriage.

I realized I wasn't the only one in Bishkek for whom university offered a welcome respite. It felt like a safe haven. We were free, at last. My guide in this new life, my role model, was Natasha. She was also Afghan, barely older than me, but already had a bachelor's degree in anthropology and human rights. She was beautiful, funny, and uninhibited. She didn't pay any attention to what others thought of her and would go out wearing dresses or shorts—whatever she felt like. She always styled her hair—which she did not cover with a headscarf, of course—and she wore nail polish in all different colors and big hoop earrings. She also had tattoos on her leg, her hand, the inside of her wrist, her back, and her neck. She was proud of these tattoos, and the poems, quotes, and drawings on her body reflected her life philosophy. She could talk about them for hours. Natasha also danced salsa and was a self-proclaimed feminist. Her mantra? *Life is too short to waste, so enjoy it!* To me, it seemed as if she'd come from another planet and couldn't possibly be Afghan. I would have never thought it possible that I could be friends with such a girl.

Natasha transformed Bishkek into my paradise. From her, I learned not to trust appearances. Her only role model in life was her older sister, Lima. Lima was completing a master's degree at Harvard. I was impressed by this because I had always wanted to go to Harvard. But I also was very struck by the way she carried herself. Lima respects herself so much, and because of this, other people do, too. She knows that she isn't less than any man, than any other person. She is a wonderful role model for Afghan women, and I certainly took her as my role model! She is a good, intelligent woman, and she made my respect for Afghan women grow. She also happened to be married to my friend Omaid from the ArtLords, and the love he demonstrates for her, too, is another thing that I very much admired. And so both sisters became very important to me.

Natasha taught me everything about my new life. She showed me how to put on makeup, what to wear, how to dance. She would organize trips outside Bishkek and birthday parties in bars. She was full of life, dreams, and talent.

"You're too serious, Zarifa! Get rid of it all, your prejudices, your worries. Live your life! Let yourself fall in love. There's nothing wrong with that!"

She seemed to speak every language and know everyone, and she introduced me to her friends, all while broadening my horizons and pushing my boundaries. We spent hours chatting at the Adriano café, our hangout spot in the city center. Most importantly, she filled me with confidence. With her, anything was possible.

One day, she introduced me to a man named Mohamed; he was really nice and worked in the city. His mother was Russian (his grandmother had been a Soviet civil servant who was posted in Bishkek and decided to stay), and his father was originally from the United Arab Emirates. He was athletic, slender, and barely taller than me; was always well-dressed; and had light-colored eyes and, above all, a big, open smile.

Mohamed spoke English, Arabic, and Russian and knew Bishkek like the back of his hand. He quickly became one of my closest friends, just like Shiraz, Samir, and Samim. He would pick me up in the evenings, and we'd go on long strolls under the trees as we talked and talked. I didn't dare even hold his hand, but these walks did me a world of good. He was surprised by my lack of life experience, or more accurately by my complete ignorance of the normal leisure activities enjoyed by girls my age, and of the general joys that were possible in life.

We would go cycling together in the parks, and he would talk to me about movies and laugh at how I didn't seem familiar with any genre but horror. It was true that my girlfriends and I mostly chose gory films that terrified us, which we watched pressed up against each other on the big sofas in the dormitory.

"I'm also going to take you to the stadium to watch a football match. It doesn't matter if you don't understand a thing, it's the atmosphere that counts!"

He strongly encouraged me to learn how to swim. I didn't want to swim alone, so I started going with the small group of female Afghan students who'd arrived in Bishkek at the same time I had. Thanks to its Soviet past, Bishkek boasts many sports facilities, including spectacular swimming pools. I, who not long ago had made fun of the women in the photos I'd seen of European beaches, didn't dare buy a swimsuit—not even a one-piece. To protect our modesty, my friends and I ended up wearing short-sleeved wet suits. After studiously watching a tutorial on YouTube several times, I quite literally took the plunge. After a few failed attempts, and after swallowing several gallons of chlorinated water, I finally did it! I floated! I swam! What a feeling.

As I became bolder in my daily life, I also continued with what Lala Kabir called my "spring-cleaning." After Mom, I now had to talk to my stepfather, Basir. I called him in Indonesia one evening. I remained calm, but I didn't beat around the bush!

"The past is weighing on me, Basir. I feel like it's holding me back. You must understand that I need to express my resentment. For years, I have filled your shoes as the head of the family for my mother, brothers, and sister because you left us. You deserted us. I took over your responsibilities, working as hard as I could to protect Mom from your family. Even now, I am still sending them money. And you've never even met your youngest son. Because of you, Mom has been rejected and is despised."

He was clearly taken by surprise and remained silent. I continued, stressing that, from then on, I wouldn't be sending any more money in his place. I had too much studying to do. When he finally spoke, he called me *bachem* (my child).

"*Bachem*, we all have our cross to bear. You have yours, that's obvious, but stop bringing up the past. Let go of it. Live in the present. Live your life."

He asked me if I needed money—it was the first time he'd ever offered—and ended up sending me what he could. He still had no visa, and it seemed like he no longer really believed in his chances of getting one, but he was making a bit of money selling *bolanis*—Afghan crepes with herbs or vegetables—in the refugee camp. After that first conversation, there came a period when we spoke more regularly, during which we were relaxed enough with one another to chat. He always seemed interested in what I was doing, and we joked around. This turned out to be another important lesson for me. When you are upset, speak up; if something hurts you, speak up.

In April 2019, with Natasha's encouragement, I volunteered to participate in an upcoming TEDx conference. TEDx events bring together a diverse range of live speakers and online contributors to exchange ideas in front of an audience.

I was the only student from the AUCA to speak at the conference; the rest of the participants were Kyrgyz. One talked about her experiences in Japan, and another was devoted to saving snow leopards from extinction. I had carefully prepared for my presentation. I knew what I wanted to say. I wanted to talk about Afghan girls, and the fate of women in my country. I had no scores to settle. I was simply happy to tell the world about where I came from; about the all-female orchestra I had left behind; about music, which I still loved with a passion; and about my journey. Just as I had done in Davos. When I'd told my mother about the upcoming event, she had asked me to translate the speech I had prepared.

"It's good, Zarifa. You must never forget you are an Afghan woman. In Afghanistan, this isn't just *your* story but also the story of countless other girls, and you need to be constantly reminding yourself of that. This story belongs to all of us."

She was right. She, too, had a complicated and painful past, one that had been stained by my country's traditions. It was interesting to see her make that point. In my opinion, this attitude was a direct result of her recent access to education. Learning to read and write had opened her eyes to the unequal status that had always defined her, and to the extent of her capabilities that, up until then, had been ignored or stifled.

To be on the safe side, she suggested I ask Aziz Royesh, a Hazara teacher and writer based in Kabul who sometimes appeared on TV, to read my speech. He was well-known, and I had a lot of respect for him. In 2015, he had even been a finalist for the Global Teacher Prize. I had met him two years before with Dr. Sarmast, when I was still studying at the ANIM, during a conference organized by the high school where Royesh taught.

After reading my speech, he gave me a couple of suggestions, as well as a warning: "Be careful, Zarifa. As soon as you open your mouth, people will dissect everything you say." And since I'd mentioned Michelle Obama in my speech, he added: "The most important thing is to remember that you are the heroine of your own story. You are your own hero. It's good to have role models, but you are the most important person. You're the one who counts."

With his advice in mind, I rewrote almost everything.

The TEDx conference was held at the Hyatt Regency in Bishkek. The decor alone impressed me; it was the fanciest hotel in the city. When I entered the room where the speeches were to be given, I saw a hundred or so people sitting on gold chairs facing the stage.

These people mostly belonged to the younger generation and were at the beginning of their professional careers. But how many others around the world were watching online? I knew my brother Ali was livestreaming the event from Kabul and was impatient to see me. There were six speakers on the lineup, and I was the first. I was also the youngest. I was so awestruck and anxious before I went on that I jumped up and down in one spot backstage to get rid of my nervous energy. Then I was up.

It was January 19, 2017. I was standing on stage, baton in my hand, and the music was about to start [. . .] The Zohra Orchestra. [. . .] The first female orchestra. Even now, two years later, when I say those words, I get the same excitement and courage as when I was standing in front of the orchestra [. . .] Many people said, "Zarifa, sometimes you forget that you are a girl." But let me tell you something: the only thing that I have never forgotten is that I am a girl. And that's my strength. That's my power.

I threw myself into speaking and everything went smoothly. I told my story and talked about my journey, my life, the risks I'd faced, and how my trials and tribulations had made me the person I was. I described how I had needed a hero and how I'd gone in search of that hero everywhere, looking to my brothers, my uncles, my male cousins, my friends . . . even celebrities. Because I never thought that a woman from my background could be a hero. As a result, I had underestimated my own capabilities. But I'd eventually learned to believe in myself anyway. I had learned how to determine what my priorities were, and what experiences and adventures I wanted to have: playing music, studying, cycling, running with my sister, dreaming, and succeeding. Succeeding in my studies, and in life. All those same things that had made me a "bad girl" with dreams that were too big for Afghanistan's patriarchal society.

Now I want to fight for girls to study music without risking their lives. I want to fight for girls to play sports anywhere and at any time, free from the fear that a man might harass them. I want to fight for girls to go to school and study. And I have found that spirit inside of me. So, find that spirit inside of you that makes you capable of achieving what you want. And that won't just spark the fire, it will inspire girls to be their own hero.

As always, once I got going, I didn't want to stop. But I had to, all the same, and after I did, I heard the applause. One by one, members of the audience came up afterward to speak with me and congratulate me. Many people approached me with questions about Afghanistan, the war, and the Taliban. "Your journey is so inspiring," one woman whispered. I was over the moon, ecstatic and touched to hear these words.

My little brother Ali had watched the whole thing from Kabul. He was proud of me, and once he got home, he gave Mom a summary of what he'd seen. He'd wanted to show her the video from the conference, but, unfortunately, it hadn't recorded properly, so he was unable to do so. But she was happy anyway because she knew that Aziz Royesh, her hero, had approved the speech. *Zarifa is evidently doing very well!* she must have thought.

Not long after the TEDx conference, all of us students gathered in the atrium on campus for our end-of-year ceremony. We had all officially qualified to pursue the four-year undergraduate curriculum and would join the first-year cohort at the start of the new academic year. I chose to major in international politics so that I could better understand the world.

This foundation year, this year of transition, had helped me to grow. I had improved my math, essay, and IT skills. I'd already had lots of confidence, but now I also had an even greater appetite for education and for life, and I'd gained a deeper faith in the future. I had learned so much about myself. I had found myself. I had always had a small light deep inside of me that I'd kept lit all this time, and now, finally, it was blazing. I had dealt with my feelings, my grudges, and the fears that had once hindered me.

I was ready to go back to Kabul for the summer holidays. I knew I would never again be the "little Zarifa" who'd been made to do everyone else's housework, blamed for everything that went wrong, and considered a burden. I was going to be reunited with the rest of the family, and I intended to continue the "spring-cleaning" I had started with Mom and Basir.

I was also launching a project whose aim was to help street children in Kabul. The project was being developed in collaboration with Bard College in New York, which had a cooperative relationship with my university in Bishkek. Every year, Bard College allocated funding for community projects, and mine had been chosen from among the applications. I'd been given four hundred dollars to set it up.

I had proposed taking care of ten children who were living in extreme poverty, for a period of several days. These were youngsters who worked on the street, whose families, if they had any, couldn't manage without their help. They sold plastic bags to shoppers in the bazaar, or pens and chewing gum to drivers, or offered to clean the drivers' windshields. But they were often also beaten up and abused.

The idea was to take them away from their tragic reality for a short while. I wanted to have them listen to music; take them to do drawing and painting with the ArtLords and Omaid; and, of course, provide them with some proper meals.

To prepare for this project, I posted an ad on Facebook to recruit volunteers who would help me supervise the children, insisting I wanted participants *from all ethnicities*. I got around fifty applications, and out of them, I chose five students who seemed to genuinely want to help these children. Everything was ready for us to get started as soon as I got back.

When I touched down in Kabul, I had an actual welcoming committee waiting for me! This was so different from my previous arrivals at the airport, which had been met with indifference or a sense of disgrace. Mom came with my sister, Najla, and my brother Ahmad was also there with my beloved niece and several of my cousins. There were around a dozen of them in total, even though getting to the airport was complicated, with all the barricades and the checkpoints, and having to wait under the hot sun. Even the roads themselves were dangerous; they were often targets for attacks. But everyone was there. Everyone embraced me and held me close. It was a real celebration.

Nonetheless, I made sure to put my headscarf back on to avoid being provocative in any way and ruining the reunion. Despite everything, as soon as we got into the cars, Mom turned to me and said: "Zarifa, your clothes are too tight, you are in Afghanistan! Also, *haan*, look how fat you've gotten. Why are you so fat?"

She was as thin as ever. Whenever she put on even the tiniest bit of weight, she did exercises at home and never failed to point out that if she had the money to better show off her appearance, we would see just how great she looked.

"Mooooooooom, stop it!"

"Okay! Okay!" she replied, hugging me again.

Najla burst out laughing. "This is great! I'm going to have some peace and quiet for at least two months. Mom will be on you and will leave me alone!"

Najla had also changed. She had gotten her hair cut very short at a men's barber to make sure the person holding the scissors would feel no hesitation about chopping off her long locks. The haircut showed off her sweet, impish face and her almond-shaped eyes. She looked like a little boy.

At home, it became clear that I was not going to fit into the orange dress my mother had sewn especially for me, so she started up with me again. "No, really, you're so young! You should exercise, look at yourself!"

Yes, it was true, I had gained a few pounds. The stress of my new life coupled with all the culinary delights Bishkek had to offer meant that I ate well, but there was no reason to panic! She kept this commentary going all evening, but we laughed about it.

She had invited my uncles and aunts to dinner. Everyone asked me questions about my life and my studies, and we chatted like a real family. Ahmad offered to teach me how to drive and, at my request, had brought me a print of the only photo we had of our father. My older sisters each invited me to spend a night at their homes. I couldn't believe it—what had happened to the fights we used to have? It was as if I had gained the respect of all the people who were living under this roof, simply by going abroad to study! Yes, I had left, but I hadn't been lost. Quite the opposite. I was finally one of them.

I did not unpack my bag until the next day. Since it was very heavy, my family undoubtedly suspected I had come bearing gifts, but they had probably expected a couple of knickknacks or some chocolates. So they were astonished when I finally opened up my treasure chest! Tennis shoes, earrings, sandals, and dresses for Najla; a backpack for Ali; coloring pencils . . . I had spent a year's worth of savings. The day before my departure, I had been simultaneously excited and anxious. How would our reunion go? Would they all be happy to see me, or would there be drama once again? Would there be a scene? Maybe that's why I had gone on a shopping spree in Bishkek, buzzing with the anticipation of spoiling and pleasing them.

Mom, who was more pragmatic, watched the others unwrap everything and frowned, saying, "Why did you spend all this money?"

But everyone was so happy with their gifts that she came around and joined in the general excitement. Najla couldn't believe it. The beautiful dress in the suitcase was for her, as were the ten or so pairs of earrings! When the family came by that afternoon to see us, Mom demanded we share the excessive gifts with our female cousins, because she wanted the family to think well of me. Ali obeyed and gave them his tennis shoes, and I also gave away some shoes that had been intended for one of my little brothers. But Najla refused to give away anything other than a single pair of earrings. Our mother gave in to her determination, rolling her eyes. Najla was untamable, just like me. What a character!

I really hoped she would one day have the opportunity to go off to university, as I had. She still dreamed of being an Olympian, but she now also wanted to become an astronomer. In the meantime, she intended to qualify for the Bamyan marathon in November.

Ali, the eldest of the boys, had grown up into a young man. Though slight of figure, he had easily taken up the mantle of responsibility and become the head of the household. He worked for a local tailor while also going to school and learning English. I was very proud of him. He had become one of my most ardent supporters at home. It would soon be his turn to apply to university.

Seeing me leave our home, our city, and even our country to study had allowed my siblings to understand that they, too, could spread their wings and fly. They already fully appreciated that education was the thing that would help them grow and flourish. That's one of my greatest sources of pride.

Even Kabul looked different to me. The place hadn't changed, yet it seemed to me to be calmer, and more welcoming. Of course, it was I who had changed, who had set my anger aside, and this meant that I could now view the world with more tolerance. I had made peace with Ahmad and all my older brothers: those with whom I shared the same absent father whose passing had hurt us so.

In addition to being occupied with my family reunion, I was also busy throwing myself fully into my project with the street children. I have to admit that the success of this little program—which, alas, lasted for far too short a time—exceeded all my expectations.

It was in this program that I met Maher, the second-born in a family of seven. Maher didn't go to school because he needed to bring home two hundred afghanis per day; if he didn't, he would be beaten with a cane by his father. Ever since he was seven years old, every day, Maher had worked at one of Kabul's many intersections, washing cars, selling plastic bags, and, if he didn't have the required sum at the end of the day, avoiding going back home. On these nights, he would sleep on the streets with four flea-ridden dogs for company. The animals would cover him with their dirty fur, keeping him warm and protecting him from thieves and drug addicts. He was so small that although he was eleven, he looked like a six-year-old.

I met Maher through an NGO named Koshana, which has taken care of some three hundred orphans and street children over the last seventeen years. How could I choose just ten kids from among them? In spite of my limited budget, I decided to take on fifteen.

Five girls and ten boys. There were fewer girls on the streets—when possible, girls' parents preferred to keep them at home and protect them from outside dangers. I took the group to ArtLords' workshops, and together we drew, painted, and colored. Little Farid, who was also eleven years old, refused to be separated from the backpack we gave him because he was afraid someone would steal it. He was so used to having to protect himself from others. Some of the children carefully set aside the food we gave them so they could share it with their siblings later. They occasionally had scars on their bodies from beatings, marks left by a life much too hard for their tender age. And they weren't spared from daily instances of other violence, either. "Sometimes people hit us with their cars on purpose," they told us.

We also played music with the children. Farid, who'd thought music was forbidden, was ecstatic. A different time, Omaid suggested they draw their dreams. Soon enough, there appeared on the pages a horse, a bright green football field (drawn by an artist who'd only experienced the dusty fields around Kabul), a power station (the dream of a child who wished not to have to live in a neighborhood that was pitch-dark at night), pink tennis shoes (for a girl who was obliged to walk barefoot), and so on.

What did I know about these children? I knew that they were part of Kabul's landscape. Children like them could be found all over the city center; everyone walks right past without seeing them. Was there really nothing we could do for them? I still had a lot to learn about my city and my country.

At home, the most spectacular transformation had to do with my mother. Our relationship was completely different now: calm and friendly. She had missed me while I was away. This was the first time I realized it, because, up until that point, we hadn't shared our feelings. Maybe some of our problems boiled down to that: all those words left unsaid had poisoned everything.

A couple of days after my return, I found her at home, sitting in the living room, bare-headed and surrounded by the little ones, who were drawing. Homayoun, the youngest at six years old, was coloring next to her. My mother had put out tea and dried fruit and had spread her notebooks and exercise books on the rugs. She was doing her homework: grammar exercises and a couple of lines of writing. It was incredible. She looked up and showed me her marks: "Look! 9/10, 10/10, 10/10, 10/10, 9/10 . . ."

She was excelling. Her pride shined through, and her joy lit up the room. Encouraged by her good grades, she had decided to keep studying. "I want to be a teacher," she announced.

I approved and applauded loudly, of course. *Go on, Mom, have at it!* So far, the family still hadn't reacted. Nobody had stood in her way; this, too, was a miracle. She was making progress by leaps and bounds.

The end of my stay was approaching. I still hadn't seen Dr. Sarmast, but we had remained in contact since I'd left the school. I was also in touch with my friends from the ANIM, like my beloved Nazira, the pale-skinned cellist from Nuristan, who would be leaving soon to go to university in West Virginia on scholarship! The violence in our country had continued to push my friends over the border and beyond: Negin had gone to India, and Shiraz was safe in Turkey while he waited for a US visa.

I hadn't seen my viola again, but I wasn't worried. When I came back from Quetta, I had given it to Dr. Sarmast, who'd gotten the broken tuning key fixed for me. When I left Kabul for university, I had entrusted the instrument to my friend Samir, who needed it for his concerts. He was the one who took care of it, and he was the only person I trusted enough to leave it in his possession.

When I left for Bishkek again, ready to start my second year at university, I felt confident, at peace with myself and my loved ones. I was serene.

The future welcomed me with open arms.

12

BELIEF IN THE FUTURE?

My second year at the American university in Bishkek had barely been impacted by the Covid-19 pandemic. But in the early summer of 2020, Kyrgyzstan feared that it, too, would be overwhelmed by the virus that had brought the planet to a standstill, and the decision was made to close its schools and universities until the situation improved. The semester had just ended, and I had really only just started to find my bearings as a student. I absolutely loved my international politics and journalism courses. During these classes, we all were constantly encouraged to think critically, to speak up, and to organize our ideas to better present them to the other students.

I had by now left the university residence hall and moved with two Afghan girlfriends into an apartment in the city. The place was located on a slightly austere Soviet housing estate. But the apartment was large and light, and close to the swimming pool and the park where I liked to walk and ride my bike. Along with my friends, I'd discovered skiing, hiking, and horseback riding.

To replace the viola, I'd taken up the ukulele, a marvelous little instrument that I carried with me everywhere. I used it to accompany myself when I sang. Music continued to be my passion, and I knew that I would be reunited with my viola someday. In the meantime, I continued to hum the tunes I had once been taught to play on it.

I was finally starting to think about the future and make concrete plans when the pandemic forced us to leave the country. In early June, we had just finished taking our last exams when the university asked foreign students to go home as soon as possible. For me, that meant returning to Kabul—even though I hadn't planned to go back that summer. Flights were filling up, and I had to hurry.

As I prepared to leave, I thought about how very far I'd come, braving brambles and thorns: from the roads of Pakistan to playing my first bars of music, the concert in Davos to my work at the radio station. Now, I almost found it difficult to see myself in the little Zarifa who'd been dragged from one house to another; who'd doubted so much; who'd constantly looked for a guide, a role model, the ghost of her father. I had so often been afraid that everything would come to an end, that I'd be sent back to square one, imprisoned in my old life once more.

I had eventually stopped searching for my father. More than his presence, I had needed an ideal. His absence had driven me to despair; it had given meaning to my sadness, provided me with a good excuse to cry. Since I'd been unable to do anything to protect myself from the malice that was sometimes aimed at me, I had transferred my angst onto my father's absence. Now, though, I had my mother, my little brothers, and my sister. And my father would forever live in my heart.

I'd breached the rules imposed by my family and society and broken the vicious cycle by refusing to get married. There is an old saying in Afghan families, *dokhtar mal e mardom asta*: "Girls are the property of other people." We are considered a commodity to be exchanged. But I had thwarted those constraints.

When I started writing this book, I went through a whole range of emotions and ambitions, swinging between elation and hopelessness: a symptom of my constant uncertainty. One day I would want to portray only the best of my country, to show that I believed in Afghanistan and was proud of its culture, its heritage, and, above all, its resilience. The following day, I would feel angry at the whole world, at the men in my country and their taste for violence, at the way women were hemmed in by our families and by our suffocating traditions.

During those months when I was writing, I remembered: each obstacle I had encountered had stopped me in my tracks, and each time I had felt a deep sense of abandonment. But with every new step, every new adventure, and above all, every encounter with a new person, I had regained my courage. Most importantly, I had eventually made peace with my family. I had freed myself from their judgment. I hoped they now understood I wasn't doing anything wrong by studying, by living a life different from the one they had intended for me.

I was now exactly where I wished to be, and I wanted to believe in my future. I still had a long way to go, but I refused to give up. I wouldn't give in.

I had just resigned myself to the idea of going back to Kabul when, one Saturday in June, I heard the news that brought my world quite literally crashing down. Natasha was dead. My free, beautiful Natasha, my heroine, had passed away. That day, a bomb placed under her car had killed her and her driver, in the middle of Kabul, as she headed to work. As custom dictated, she would be buried the same day. I wouldn't be there. Her photo with her huge smile appeared on Twitter and Facebook alongside the words that announced her death. My heart broke, shattered into pieces.

I found myself speaking to her: *Natasha, the first thing I asked myself was whether you suffered. I fear that above all else. At the Adriano café back in Bishkek, you would often say: "I want to live. I don't want to die, especially not in an explosion!" You used to be furious when you said that, as if you didn't quite believe such a thing was possible. And then we'd laugh about it: "Oh no, no way, we won't end up like that!" Did we think we could ward off bad luck? I already miss you so much . . . How will I go on without you? Do you remember how whenever something bad happened, I'd try to convince myself that there had to be a reason for it, one that we wouldn't find right away, but that would one day make it all make sense? Well, this time, I won't be convinced. Because this time, sense doesn't come into it.*

Natasha's tragic death shook our student community to its core. On the eve of the holidays, university officials prepared a memorial ceremony and asked me to write something in her honor. She had been one of their brightest students, graduating with a double bachelor's degree the previous year. They shared in our grief and wanted to pay tribute.

Natasha was twenty-four years old at the time of her death. Those of us she left behind were gripped as much by anger as by pain. The letter I read during the ceremony was a heartbreaking testimony to our suffering. Natasha's passing had left us distraught, and her untimely death sent a hopeless signal: nothing had changed in Afghanistan. It was clear that the country was still sinking into a nightmare.

Her parents had requested she come back to Kabul after she graduated. Even her sister, Lima, now consumed by pain and remorse in the United States, had urged her to return to her parents. Without difficulty, Natasha, a young multilingual graduate, had secured a job at the Afghanistan Independent Human Rights Commission in Kabul. This decision was probably what had cost her her life.

What freedom had her killers been trying to crush? Had they been attempting to target the commission through her, or were they directly targeting the rebellious, educated woman who danced the salsa and refused to be censored? When they killed her, they killed the need for kindness, friendship, equality—the reason we are alive—that so many of us in and from Afghanistan feel; they killed our dreams of freedom, justice, and peace. They killed our hopes. And they continue to kill our country.

The investigation promised by the authorities, as per usual, didn't progress—was the case even looked into? After Natasha's death, I

realized that numerous educated young people, qualified women, journalists, and human rights activists were being murdered every week.
Nobody ever claims responsibility for these killings. The authorities
condemn the violence. Yet no one really seems to want to put a stop to
this madness.

The night before she died, we had spent two hours talking on the
phone. Natasha was in Kabul, and I was in Bishkek. That evening, she
talked at length about her disappointment and exasperation, and about
the results of her return to her country. She denounced the offensive
behavior of the men who would whistle at her in the street, as well as
the insolent women with their judgmental looks and biting comments.
And the threats. Always there were threats. Against women. Against the
city. Against anyone working to promote human rights. Natasha wanted
to leave quickly and go to the US to complete her master's degree. She
couldn't handle this restrictive atmosphere anymore. She had applied
for a new scholarship to continue her studies and training abroad. She
would have gotten it; of that, I am sure.

In an article printed in the *New York Times*, her friend Mujib
Mashal, the daily's correspondent in Afghanistan, found the perfect
words to describe the death machine that continued to work against the
young Afghans who were trying to defy the country's violent past and
aspire to the future: "She joins a painfully long list of young Afghans
who died trying to help their country." He also didn't fail to mention
how Natasha outdanced everyone on the dance floor.

Natasha was gone. Just like so many other friends, neighbors, and
acquaintances who had been killed in attacks and explosions. So many
loved ones had already passed away during the course of my short life.
I thought of Sami, who didn't survive the attack on the American university campus in 2016, and of another friend who was killed in July
2016 by a fatal explosion during a Hazara protest that was organized to
demand "light," or electricity, for the Bamyan valley, and so many more.

I'm angry at our parents, our grandparents, and their forefathers, who left us a country that is eternally at war, who left us explosions, and bombs, and rockets. They brought us into a world in which we can die in a blink of an eye, for nothing. Is this our future?

I know you would wrinkle your nose, Natasha, if you heard me moaning and cursing like this. "You're lucky I'm far away!" you would scold whenever I complained during those last months. "All the more reason to hang on." That's what you would have said. Despite my grief.

It's up to the younger generation, my generation—including the ones who can access higher education, albeit with difficulty—to stand up and prevent the Taliban from stamping out our hard-won rights. I want to be strong like Natasha, like Lima. We girls, especially, must help and support each other, must keep ourselves and our friends from being sent back to the homes of our fathers or to husbands. There are still far too many people in Afghanistan who would prefer to keep us there.

If there is still a country where the word "feminist" must find meaning, it's Afghanistan. Afghan women need to learn to show solidarity, to fight together, shoulder to shoulder if necessary, with like-minded men. Not just for our own sake, but for the sake of our sisters and mothers. The more educated we women become, the more we can teach and train others.

After all, it's all about respect. Not the respect men think they are showing us by hiding us away from other men, or by always referring to us as the wives, daughters, mothers, and even nieces of a man, instead of calling us by our own names. It is said that they do these things in order to protect men's honor, though what they are actually doing is using religion to justify their misogyny.

No. I am talking about the kind of respect every human being deserves, the kind that is shared among equals. I want to be able to walk down the street with my scarf around my neck without being harassed. I want to be able to drive a car or ride a bicycle or a motorcycle. I accept the risk of being branded a "bad girl" that goes with trying to achieve this. We are not asking for privileges; we are just asking to be treated as equals. Remember, this is a country where women are still considered to be "half-brains" by the most archaic mullahs. And this isn't just about music, either; women have to fight harder than men in all fields. That's what matters: giving women a voice, and then that voice being raised so that it may be heard.

My mother is already on the right track. She continues her studies, despite the fact that the Uncles have become angry with her over it on more than one occasion and have accused her of abandoning her children.

"Your kids are running wild. You should be at home, taking care of them and cooking for them," grumbled Haider one day when the youngest played downstairs in the courtyard.

Strangely enough, it's my mother who gets picked on, but no one in the family thinks to remind Basir, still in Indonesia, of his responsibilities as a father and husband. He still criticizes me sometimes by telling my mom about a dress or pose he's seen on my Facebook page that he deems too provocative.

To encourage my mother, I tell her over and over again just how proud I am of her: "It's really good to see you so determined, not paying attention to all the gossip, or the chatter."

But she doesn't need others' approval; she is proud of herself, and that's enough. She knows what she is worth. All she wants is for us to get an apartment together when I finish my studies and return to Kabul for good. She just wants to live her life. Even when she faced adversity, some part of her never doubted that she might deserve better, and that same conviction was what drove me as well. Here is what I believe to be true: if you *can* do better, then you *must* do better. Life isn't worth living if you're not constantly striving to find your destiny.

Before her death, Natasha's favorite poem was "Still I Rise" by the American poet Maya Angelou, whom she greatly admired. She could recite it by heart and loved one line, in particular: "Does my sassiness upset you?"

I hope so. I hope our sassiness will forever be an upsetting force. I hope it disrupts Afghan men and shakes them up. It is this sassiness that will carry Afghanistan and its people, especially its women, into the future.

For Afghan women, progress is slow and the mountain is steep. We constantly have to overcome the prejudices of our society and the fears of our parents. Yes, we are strong enough to do that. And also, we are tired. And we cannot count on other countries to help us. We have not even been able to count on our own government. That is why I have for so long felt that we must change things ourselves. The women of Afghanistan. The artists and the creators. My generation, both the boys and the girls. And yet, like so many of my friends, I fear that the ultraconservative forces in our society who hate us—hate women, hate educated young people—will seize the reins of power once more. I fear that the Taliban will reimpose their archaic laws and cover us back up with burkas.

And I'm afraid that one day, just as we are angry at our parents, it will be our children's turn to be angry at us.

AFTERWORD

WHAT IS LEFT OF OUR HOPE?

On the afternoon of August 15, 2021, I'm getting ready to leave for the English class I'm teaching to Kyrgyz and Russian students in Kyrgyzstan, when I get the call from my brother Ali.

"Zarifa, the Taliban are in Kabul."

I don't believe him. I don't want to believe it.

Other cities have fallen, of course: one by one, without much resistance, as if the Afghan army had simply evaporated. But Kabul? A quick glance at the news is enough. Yes, they are there. They are very near our neighborhood in the west of the city, where my mother still lives with my sister and brothers. And they are making progress, heading for the city center. The president and his government have fled. The army is no more. Gone for good.

I immediately see my little sister Najla's face superimposed over the distressed messages my Afghan friends are posting on Facebook. I can't imagine her, of all people—in the throes of her own rebellion, determined to make her dreams a reality—living under the yoke of the Taliban. No more than I can imagine my mother doing so: my mother, who already survived their brutal occupation back in 1996, but who, this time, is alone with her children, with no one to protect her. And what about all my friends who are journalists, musicians, students? What will become of them?

I leave to go teach my class but find myself unable to concentrate. I'm glued to the news from Afghanistan, struggling to hold back my tears.

When I get home, I shut myself in the bathroom and cry for a long time. I don't know what else to do; I feel so helpless I can barely think.

The Taliban have taken down the black, green, and red Afghan flag and replaced it everywhere with their own white banner covered in Islamist slogans. Afghanistan, my country, no longer exists. It has been pushed aside by the sinister "Islamic Emirate" of the turbaned, sandal-clad fighters. My own distressing experiences and personal suffering are now joined by a new pain, a new loss: that of my homeland, my anchor in this world, a place I had so hoped to help change one day and that now seems lost forever . . .

On Facebook, I'm stunned to see that some people are expressing their support for the new regime, in the name of communitarianism. How is it acceptable to them that the Taliban now presides over the destinies of all Afghan men and, worse, Afghan women? How can we forgive the Taliban's crimes and the terror attacks our generation has suffered? I understand that Afghans are tired of war, tired of violence, tired of the land mines and the fighting. But this is too high a price to pay.

I tremble to think about what will happen to all those I love, and to all the women and girls of Afghanistan.

Over the next few days, foreign reporters start to contact me. Dr. Sarmast has given them my name, as well as the names of five of my fellow students at the ANIM, including two boys who are currently studying in the United States, so that we may act as spokespersons for the music school.

Will the Taliban once again outlaw music? In any case, the first restrictions are already being put in place: no more live music, no concerts, and the radio stations are only permitted to broadcast religious songs. And the restrictions are not limited to music. As soon as the Taliban came to power, they began to paint over the ArtLords' huge murals in the streets of Kabul, and to blur out their slogans.

My first interviews are dominated by emotion and grief. When I talk to Dr. Sarmast, I describe my despair. *We've lost everything.*

His words comfort me. *The music school is stronger than the Taliban think. This school will continue to resist, even if we can't play in Afghanistan.* When we hang up, I'm able to convince myself that there is still hope for the ANIM and its musicians, even if it's hard to hang on to that hope. And perhaps there is also still hope for my sister and my mother. My mother's experience with the Taliban when she was a teenager was very hard on her, and frightened her. I worry about Najla, who dreams so big, whose light is so bright. I worry for my brothers, too: especially about the dangers of them being exposed to Taliban extremism. But I worry most of all for the women in my family. I feel angry that they have to face all of this, especially since I had hoped that we were moving into a time when Afghanistan's beauty could be more clearly seen again, and its women could be free.

Over time, my anger doesn't fade. I'm angry at our corrupt government, who abandoned us, but also at the rest of the world, who seem to have forgotten the dreams and hopes of my generation. I am heartbroken to see how the entire world has seemingly turned their backs on us.

The situation is impossible. But we mustn't give up hope, give in.

Despite their brutality, the Taliban—who have shown that they haven't changed in the last twenty years—are not, in the first months after taking Kabul, able to silence Afghanistan. Women continue to demonstrate their sheer bravery and extraordinary courage by protesting in various cities, just as they have in Kabul. They take the lead at these marches to demand the right to work, the right to go to school and university. They stand up for their rights, despite the guns pointed at their heads.

But also, the thing I have always feared has happened: no men have gone out to stand beside these brave women in the streets of Kabul. Women chant for justice, all alone. It seems everyone in the world has put on blindfolds, or chosen not to see what is happening in my home country.

The Afghan journalists filming these demonstrators are arrested and brutally beaten. Their battered bodies attest to the violence of these attacks. "We could have beheaded you," their tormentors tell them, the final insult before letting the journalists go.

At the same time, the black turbans appear on television to state that women cannot run government ministries; this task would be beyond them, they say, and, besides, women's place is in the home, where they are to have and raise children and educate them according to the laws of Islam.

Do not misunderstand me: I believe Islam is a beautiful religion. I am Muslim, too. But I do not believe that in making these demands the Taliban is truly representing Islam. They have closed schools for girls. For women, sports are now out of the question. They do not allow women to go to work. They unleash violence and terror on my country, in front of the entire world. They are terrorists. They are using Islam as a tool to justify whatever they are doing.

It only took a few days, after that day in August 2021, for our world to fall apart.

I learn that at Radio Jawanan, my radio station, the manager Hamida decided to temporarily take her female colleagues off the air, to protect her team. Ultimately, though, they are not allowed to return for long. A few women can come to the television studios, provided they cover everything but their eyes and broadcast only programs that conform with the Taliban's interpretation of Sharia—rules and regulations based on the Quran that outline how men and women are supposed to live.

Each new announcement regarding the formation of the new government and the laws that now govern Afghanistan turns my stomach. The country is going backward, retreating into the darkness, and risks dragging an entire generation down along with it: a generation of young people who thought they could finally believe in their future.

Though I am discouraged, I refuse to believe that all these years spent fighting for a small parcel of freedom were for nothing. It is impossible to know what tomorrow will bring. To avoid succumbing to despair, I imagine the Zohra Orchestra playing in front of the cliffs that protect the Buddhas of Bamyan, in central Afghanistan—the girls dancing and singing before those silent giants. I dream of an Afghanistan at peace, where I can sit in a café and laugh with my friends Samim, Shiraz, and Samir.

Where Najla, who used to run circuits on our rooftop and practice football, can play sports competitively and enroll in university.

Where my mother can go back to school and become a teacher. Where she can come to listen to me play the viola without fear, and where I can take her to visit the ocean, like I always dreamed I would, and see her lift up the hem of her dress and dip her feet in the water.

Where Ali, who goes to such lengths to perfect his English, gets a break, without having to choose between the army or a militia.

I cling to these images in my mind's eye, and they help me remain standing. The turbans and Kalashnikovs invading the streets of Kabul cannot kill all hope.

◆　◆　◆

When I finished the first draft of my book in 2019, I concluded it by saying how much I feared the Taliban coming back to power. And then in 2021—after my book was written, but before it was published—I added what I'd thought and felt after the Taliban entered Kabul.

Today, in 2023, the changes that I feared have become reality.

Is it the end? I kept asking this question. At first, I found no answers.

But then I remember the girl I once was: little Zarifa, who lived only miles from each bomb blast ordered and sent to Kabul by the Taliban. She lost friends to those blasts, and still she held on to the power of hope and overcame everything that was thrown her way to block her dreams: attempts to stop her from going to university, from holding and playing her viola, from believing she could make a better life for her mother and her siblings, and for many others like her.

The little Zarifa I remember fought to overcome, and today, at the age of twenty-four, she has achieved most of those dreams. I am that Zarifa.

I still owe it to little Zarifa to go to Harvard, to help as many girls as I can to go to school and university, to become a louder voice for my fellow Afghan sisters who are voiceless today under the Taliban regime. The journey for women in Afghanistan is tougher today than it has ever been.

I remember that I have barely started my journey, that I must hold on to hope even tighter than before, be more rebellious than ever. I tell myself: *Zarifa, you have a long way to go. Stay tall and proud.*

And best of luck!

ACKNOWLEDGMENTS

Firstly, I would like to thank Sammi Cannold: Thank you, Sammi! Thank you for helping my family leave Afghanistan.

Thank you to the team at the Andrew Lloyd Webber Foundation, and to Christa D'Souza, for doing so much good in a world where kindness is rare.

Maha, you have not been just my aunt but my role model, my support, and my best friend through everything. Thank you!

Anne Chaon, thank you for giving me the chance to tell my story and for all your kindness these past few years.

Lala Kabir, thank you for being there for me when it mattered. You are the family I have chosen myself, and how lucky I was to have you.

Lima and Omaid, thank you for introducing me to Natasha, and for all of your support.

Jennifer Moberg, thank you for helping me to visit Yale and the United States.

Chris Stone, thank you for the violin, and for being there for me during some of the most difficult periods of my life.

Thanks to Shari MacDonald Strong, my beautiful friend Emmanuelle Hardouin in Paris, Lauren Wendelken and Neyla Downs in New York, and to everyone at Susanna Lea Associates, for supporting my book and helping me to get the words just right.

And thanks to some precious souls who made life a little more beautiful: Sonia, Hanae, Maryam, Hasina, Samir, Samim, Shiraz, Attila, and so many others that I cannot name you all.

ADDITIONAL RESOURCES

Chapter 1

The Zohra concert at Davos. https://www.youtube.com/watch?v=hyBoW-UxWIEQ. (Zarifa comes on stage at 13:22, after the introductions.)

Chapter 3

The "bad girl" video. https://www.youtube.com/watch?v=ZJlu9lCz_Zw&t=30s.

Chapter 12

Article about the death of Natasha Khalil: Mashal, Mujib. "Another Young Leader Taken. Afghans Ask: How Many More?", the *New York Times,* June 30, 2020: https://www.nytimes.com/2020/06/29/world/asia/afghanistan-women-human-rights.html.

Other

Video of Zarifa Adiba's first experience conducting: "Dohktar Astam" ("I Am a Girl"), performed in 2016 in celebration of International Girl Child Day. https://www.youtube.com/watch?v=AKJueNp4rHg.

ABOUT THE AUTHORS

Zarifa Adiba is the lead violist and co-conductor of Zohra, Afghanistan's first (and only) all-female orchestra. She studied at the Afghanistan National Institute of Music, the only music education entity in Afghanistan, for three years. She is currently studying International Politics at both Bard College and American University of Central Asia. She is an activist for girls and education and has participated in several panels, including at the World Economic Forum in 2017. *Playing for Freedom* is her first book.

Anne Chaon is a journalist and former correspondent for the Agence France-Presse. She was based in Kabul, Afghanistan, from June 2016 to September 2018 and again in June 2021.